MOUNTAIN BIKING
Colorado's Front Range

Front Range Ride Location Map

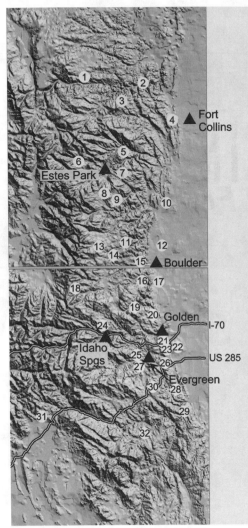

1. Seven Mile Creek
2. Hewlett Gulch
3. Flowers Road/Monument Gulch
4. Lory State Park/Horsetooth Mountain Park
5. Crosier Mountain
6. Fall River Road
7. Pole Hill Road
8. Pierson Park Road
9. Johnny Park
10. Rabbit Mountain
11. James Creek
12. Boulder Reservoir
13. Sourdough Trail
14. Switzerland Trail
15. Betasso Preserve
16. Walker Ranch
17. Community Ditch
18. Rollins Pass
19. Golden Gate Canyon State Park
20. White Ranch Park
21. Apex Park
22. Wm. F. Hayden Green Mountain Park
23. Matthews/Winters Park
24. Idaho Springs and Central City Rides
25. Elk Meadow Park
26. Mount Falcon Park
27. Alderfer/Three Sisters Park
28. Deer Creek Canyon Park
29. Waterton Canyon/Colorado Trail
30. Meyer Ranch Park
31. Colorado Trail at Kenosha Pass
32. Buffalo Creek Mountain Bike Area

MOUNTAIN BIKING
Colorado's Front Range

Great Rides in and around
Fort Collins, Denver, and Boulder

by Derek Ryter and Jarral Ryter

PRUETT PUBLISHING COMPANY
BOULDER, COLORADO

Printed in the United States
10 9 8 7 6 5 4 3 2 1

Library of Congress Cataloging-in-Publication data

    Ryter, Derek.
        Mountain biking Colorado's Front Range : great rides
    in and around Fort Collins, Denver, and Boulder /
    by Derek Ryter and Jarral Ryter.
        p.   cm.
    Includes bibliographical references (p.) and index.
    ISBN 0-87108-890-8 (pbk.)
    1. All terrain cycling—Front Range (Colo. and Wyo.)—
Guidebooks. 2. Front Range (Colo. and Wyo.)—Guidebooks.
I. Ryter, Jarral, 1968– . II. Title.
GV1045.5.F76R98   1998
796.6'3'097886—dc21   98-23659
                                     CIP

Cover and book design by Kathleen McAffrey, Starr Design
Book composition by Lyn Chaffee
Cover photograph by Eric Wunrow, White Ranch Park near Golden.
Interior photographs by the authors except where noted otherwise
Maps and elevation profiles by Derek Ryter

Contents

PREFACE

*D*enver and its surrounding area are experiencing an economic boom in the mid-1990s, and growth is occurring at a rate seen only a few times before in the region's history, including its gold rushes and real estate booms. You will undoubtedly see evidence of this in the city itself and on the interstate highways that traverse the state—usually when you try to reach recreation areas.

Mountain biking, too, has changed through the 1980s and 1990s, from a backyard sport to a multimillion-dollar industry. For some, mountain biking is a profession, for others a weekend pastime. Many mountain bikers, like the authors of this book, love to ride because of the physical challenge and the feeling of traveling through the forest free of the confines of a heavy steel shell and the noise of motorized off-road vehicles—though avoiding the latter is not always possible. We produced this book with the intention of providing a different view of mountain bike rides: a user-friendly guide with historic references and geologic background to help you learn more about the Front Range area and become more of a part of it.

As you drive the crowded highways to the trails around the Front Range that wind through tracts of private land, give thanks to Coloradans of the past who donated and sold land to the parks that have preserved it for use by all. These include Jack Moomaw, who worked to preserve Rabbit Mountain Park; the Soderberg family, who sold their ranch to Larimer County for Horsetooth Mountain Park; and the Spencer Wyant family, who greatly affected the Jefferson County open space park program, and Alderfer/Three Sisters Park in particular. The Walker and White families were also instrumental in getting the two parks that bear their names going. The

Meyer family is responsible for Meyer Ranch Open Space Park. The Hayden family donated or sold to the state most of the land that is now the William Frederick Hayden Green Mountain Park. This is certainly not an exhaustive list. Anyone who has sold land to the state and individual counties instead of to developers or casinos should be held in high regard.

Colorado taxpayers who over the years have voted and paid for park land purchases, trail construction, park management, and preservation of historical sites, must be thanked as well. Finally, remember that the state lottery also provides funding for parks at different levels.

The authors are natives of southwestern Colorado and are not accustomed to seeing vast tracts of land tied up by private interests, as is unfortunately the case on the Front Range. This is one reason we so value the parks systems within Colorado and hope public lands can grow in acreage as our population increases. We believe in responsible use of the last wild areas of Colorado and will emphasize this throughout the book. We also believe that with responsible use of wilderness areas, mountain biking will be allowed for years to come, regardless of population growth.

ACKNOWLEDGMENTS

We would first like to thank Jodi and Anne for helping out and being patient. We would also like to thank all the folks we spoke with around the area while riding and looking for rides. This includes the staffs of various bike shops as well as other cyclists.

This book required a good measure of high-tech assistance as well as the physical effort of riding the trails. Invaluable technical assistance was provided by John Sowl, Paul Morrison, Bill Lugsch, and the Internet. Digital elevation-model data was provided free of charge (if you download it) by the United States Geological Survey (we would like to thank Congress for not eliminating this agency) and no help at all was provided by Trek USA Bicycles, though we still ride them. Trail input was provided by Jeff Sanders and Todd Murray.

Historical references were provided by various Colorado parks, and by a handy book, *Central City and Gilpin County: Then and Now*, by Robert L. Brown and the Denver Public Library. James McTighe's *Roadside History of Colorado* is another reference that provides quick information when traveling around the state. Though there are a good number of geologic references on Colorado, more than should ever be mentioned in a cycling book, Halka Chronic's *Roadside Geology of Colorado* gives a cursory view of geology in the state in language that most can understand.

COLORADO'S FRONT RANGE: A MOUNTAIN BIKER'S MECCA

*I*f Moab, Utah, is mountain biking's capital, then Colorado's Front Range is the sport's Mecca. The region's naturally diverse terrain offers mountain bikers beauty, challenge, and access—a combination rivaled by few places on earth.

This guide covers some of the best trails the Front Range has to offer, all of which are easily accessible from the Denver metro area, and several of which are within a few minute's drive (or ride) from Fort Collins, Boulder, Colorado Springs, and areas in between. We have described the terrain, length, and difficulty of each trail so you can plan trips according to the workout you want or the scenery you'd like to explore. Each trail description features historical and geological information that may generate further interest in particular areas. Above all, we hope this guide encourages readers to practice nonmotorized recreation by describing some of the many great places in this state that are better seen from a bike saddle than an automobile seat.

Front Range Physiography

Colorado's Front Range is part of the central Rocky Mountains. It marks the western boundary of the Great Plains in northern Colorado. To the south, the Great Plains are broken by the Wet Mountains (where you'll find Pikes Peak) and, farther south, the Spanish Peaks. In this book, we refer to the Front Range and the foothills of the Rockies separately, though they are both part of the same geologic phenomenon. The foothills consist of tilted and broken sedimentary rocks of the Great Plains that form hogbacks, as well as the eroded remnants of uplifted igneous and metamorphic rocks.

Places like the town of Morrison, Red Rocks Amphitheater, Rabbit Mountain Park, and Lory State Park are located in the foothills. The towns of Evergreen, Idaho Springs, and Estes Park are in the Front range itself.

With such gifts as lode-gold deposits in the mountains, the Dakota Ridge dinosaur tracks, Denver Basin oil, Lyons flagstone, and (most recently) a burgeoning outdoor recreation industry, the uplifted Rocky Mountains have delivered immeasurable wealth: The ski areas alone now bring in more money than was ever made during the historic gold rushes. But long before we were around to measure wealth in terms of dollars and things that glitter, the Rocky Mountains were busy forming themselves, changing from ocean to land mass, heaving and uplifting, as if to prepare for our arrival with skis, hiking boots, and mountain bikes in hand. After the Front Range was uplifted, it was dissected by running water while the alpine valleys above it were being smoothed by glaciers. The water cutting into the relatively hard metamorphic and igneous rocks that form the core of the uplift produced the chasms that we drive through on virtually every highway that ventures westward.

The rock is fractured in a regular manner that is evident when we drive up canyons or go rock climbing. In the canyon walls, fractures can be seen with distinct sets of orientations—some vertical and trending north-south, others occurring at steep angles and trending in other directions. These fractures are responsible for mineral deposits because they provide a conduit for mineral-rich water. They also create weaknesses in rock slopes and cliffs that lead to rockfalls and rock slides, especially after heavy rains. Fractures also provide conduits for groundwater to move through the impervious rock to underground wells used for domestic water. This has a downside, in that water contaminated with human or industrial waste is carried quickly through the fractures to the wells.

A number of mineral deposits, including gold, silver, copper, zinc, iron, and lead, are related to the uplift of the Front Range. Evidence of mineralization can be seen in the red-stained rocks along Clear Creek from the Colorado School of Mines in Golden west to the mines around Idaho Springs and beyond. The prospect of mineral deposits attracted miners to other parts of the Front Range, including Central City and Nederland and the Poudre Canyon up-stream from Fort Collins. The Gilpin County area, named after the first governor of the Colorado Territory, was the site of the first lode-gold discovery in Colorado. The discovery was made by John Gregory near Black Hawk, and a couple of the rides in this book explore this area.

Front Range Climate

The weather along the Front Range is a mix of mountain and plains weather but is milder than either because it is located in the rain shadow created by the mountains. The cold fronts that ravage the plains and Midwest generally only graze this area. The most significant weather-related hazard is lightning. In the United States, Colorado is second only to Florida in the number of lightning strikes it receives in a year, so keep an eye out for thunderheads building over the mountains and moving out onto the plains.

Spring weather can be wet, with heavy snows falling into April. Summer high temperatures average from eighty to ninety degrees in the foothills and are ten to fifteen degrees cooler at elevations above 10,000 feet. Afternoon thunderstorms are common between May and September. The good thing about the thunderstorms is that although they normally form along the foothills, they don't get really big until they get out over the plains east of Denver. The bad thing is that they grow very quickly over the mountains and are very dangerous. In the event you are caught in a thunderstorm, stay off ridges and peaks, but also be aware that flash floods can occur during torrential thunderstorms.

The cycling season for many trails can begin as early as May, lasting through the summer and into autumn. Autumn can be very dry and good for riding—if you can pull yourself away from the Broncos games, of course—though you must be careful not to get caught in snowstorms that can develop suddenly on September afternoons. It is not uncommon for mountain bikers to get caught in snowstorms in the high country and suffer from hypothermia, while in Denver the temperature is a comfortable sixty-five degrees. So be prepared for cold weather by packing a waterproof jacket, an extra energy bar, and by making certain that your bike is maintained and ready to get you back to warmer elevations. Adjust your equipment to meet the demands of each ride by studying the elevation and ride descriptions in each chapter.

Aside from sudden cloudbursts and lightning, another common weather-related hazard is wind. The Front Range is a major orographic (related to mountains) factor in weather patterns, and its canyons funnel winds down onto the plains. At virtually any time of year on the Front Range, winds can exceed 100 miles per hour in any particular location. In the fall and winter this can cause downslope air movement and resulting chinook winds that make cities like Boulder twenty degrees warmer than those farther east along the Platte River. Conversely, when you are out in the fall or winter, and the sun begins to go down, the cold wind can be brutal. In mountain biking, wind is not as much of a problem as it is in road riding, but be aware that the good time you are making on the way out may be influenced by a tailwind that could well be your nemesis on the way back.

With the high winds and altitude and low humidity of the region, dehydration can be a problem on rides. Take at least two water bottles, and if you are running low on water, it might be a good idea to skip that last loop at White Ranch. Pack some snacks and energy bars to help you refuel. Remember that dehydration and low blood sugar can impair your motor skills, your ability to concentrate on the trail, and your judgment. It can also compromise your ability to deal with hypothermia if you get caught in an early- or late-season snowstorm. Listen to your body and your common sense.

Off-Road Cycling: Dos and Don'ts and Other Tips

Though this book is not meant to be a tutor on off-road cycling, there are a few guidelines that should be mentioned in case you haven't spent much time on technical terrain.

Equipment

First of all, your equipment has to be ready for tough climbs and rough descents. We would rather not suggest a particular brand or component group because different product lines change quickly as bike manufacturers downgrade the components in a line, supposedly to stay competitive in the price range. Visit a bike shop that offers advice and suggestions and that will educate you on what makes sense for your skill level, and then you decide if you can afford it. We would, however, like to say that good, solid components will make a significant difference in your comfort, ability, and overall enjoyment. Your bike can make the difference between cleaning a climb or technical stretch and walking.

A high-end mountain bike is, by definition, a bike ready for competition and is equipped with a component group of Shimano Deore XT or LX, the XT being the higher end of the two. The STX group is below the Deore LX and there are several groups that fall below it. For most of the rides in this book, an STX group or better will suffice, though smaller cyclists will do fine with a sub-STX component group. If you ride hard and/or prefer technical and steep trails, we recommend riding a higher end mountain bike.

You don't need a high-end mountain bike with any kind of suspension, but good brakes and shifters are a must. You also don't need a super lightweight bike, but keep in mind that high-quality bikes, usually less than 30 pounds, make rides a lot more fun, and the bike will last a lot longer.

The authors have opted for fairly high-end bikes mostly because we have suffered through broken derailleurs, bent rims, and lugging the heavy frames that were available ten years ago over mountain passes. By avoiding unsafe and unreasonable trails, we have helped our bikes last a long time with few costly repairs.

Pack the right equipment and tools. Remember that even on short rides, forgetting any one of several important items can make an outing miserable.

Equipment that should accompany every ride:
- Spare tube
- Patch kit
- Pump
- Chain tool (may be part of multiple-tool kit)
- Tire tools
- Allen wrenches (at least four and six millimeter; may be part of multiple-tool kit)

- Small first-aid kit
- Extra energy bar

Optional equipment:
- Spoke wrench
- Ten-millimeter wrench
- Six-inch adjustable wrench
- Cell phone (though most rides are out of range)
- Spare chain links

Carrying your bike back to the car even a short distance is no fun. So keep your bike well stocked with a mounted pump and saddle pouch (keeping your tools on your bike will help you remember to take them along), and check your equipment and tools regularly.

We recommend taking a spare tube as well as a tube-patch kit because some holes cannot be patched. You should become familiar with how to use a chain tool and also carry extra links. *Chain suck* or a bad shift in the wrong situation can break or twist your chain, requiring immediate attention. Tire tools make fixing flats much quicker, and some tires are almost impossible to get off without one.

Your first-aid kit can contain as little as a roll of gauze and ointment, because the most common mountain biking injuries are scrapes and gashes. This means that blood loss can be a problem, so make sure you know first-aid procedures for dealing with bleeding before you take off for a remote destination.

A ten-millimeter wrench is handy for adjusting brakes, and a six-inch adjustable wrench can take care of a lot of miscellaneous small repairs. A multiple-purpose biking tool kit will normally include Allen wrenches, a chain tool, a spoke wrench, and variously sized wrenches. A spoke wrench can help make sure you ride back in case you bend a rim or knock one way out of true.

All these items fit easily into a small saddle pouch and, collectively, can get you out of just about any cycling mishap. There are a number of good instruction manuals on bike repair and maintenance, including one of our favorites, *Bicycling Magazine's Basic Maintenance and Repair* by the editors of *Bicycling* magazine. Stop in your local bike shop if you have questions; some shops even offer free classes on bike repair.

Good cycling or sporting shades can act as eye protection when rocks and branches are flying around, but remember that your dark lenses may be good in the bright sun yet also make the trail hard to see when you ride into the well-shaded forest. Thus, choice of lenses in cycling eyewear can be important. In some areas, such as a trail that goes in and out of shade, or when the sky is cloudy, yellow lenses work well. When light is very dim, clear lenses are optimal. Your prescription eyeglasses will provide some protection, though they will not keep the drying wind off your eyes.

Quality cycling gloves help absorb shock and, what is more important, protect your palms when you crash. Full gloves made of heavy Lycra and leather can help to keep your fingers warm when the weather turns cold.

Other cycling gear includes helmets, jerseys, jackets, shorts, and shoes. A good helmet is one that fits comfortably and doesn't bounce around when you ride rough trails. It will also cover the sides of your head and your forehead. Don't worry about aerodynamics while mountain biking, just try to protect your melon. It is simply foolhardy to ride in any terrain without wearing an approved helmet.

Cycling jerseys are not essential but provide pockets for food or other essentials and usually fit very well. Some jerseys are made for hot or cool weather. Jackets come in many different styles, but we like the lightweight windproof variety when cool temperatures are of concern and the waterproof and breathable variety in wet weather. Remember that it's easy to become too warm and to sweat excessively if your cycling jacket is heavy.

Cycling shorts can make a big difference when it comes to comfort because they incorporate padding and form-fitting style. Loose-fitting shorts equipped with padding are also available.

Good-quality mountain biking shoes are recommended because of the added power and control they make possible. Even if you do not use clipless pedals, a mountain bike shoe with a stiff sole will transfer more power to the pedal and help your feet stay on the pedals on rough trails.

Off-Road Cycling Techniques

Most mountain biking can be broken down into two types: climbing and descending. These two types of riding have some basic similarities and some major differences. For mountain biking in general, though, there are some techniques that can help you ride better.

First, when riding, don't follow other bikes too closely. If you do, you will start to watch the wheel in front of you, and when the other cyclist swerves to miss a large rock or cactus, you won't see it until it's too late. If you are right on the wheel of the person in front of you and they get stuck on a steep climb, you will have to slow down, ruining your chances of cleaning the climb. If you are following at a short distance, though, you can watch other cyclists ahead of you as they ride through technical spots. In a way that is similar to watching your golfing partner putt on a green, you can learn a lot from how your cycling partner fares on the chosen climb route, descent, or stream crossing.

"For every uphill, there's an equal and opposite downhill"—Technical Trails

On many rides, the trail will drop or round a corner and cross a small creekbed before coming to a steep rocky climb, and it may catch you unaware. Other trails will climb more steadily, and the upcoming ascent will be apparent. When riding in an area like Deer Creek or the Colorado Trail, you must keep an eye on the upcoming trail in order to anticipate a steep climb. As the climb approaches, make sure you are in the proper front chain ring, because the front derailleur will have trouble pulling the chain off big rings when you are cranking. To chose the proper chain ring, get a feel for your speed, ability, and the steepness of the upcoming trail. If the uphill climb is short and your speed is good, you may stay in your middle ring. If the climb looks very technical and long, you may want to drop into your smallest gear and shift the rear derailleur onto a smaller gear as well so that you aren't spinning like crazy before you get to the hard part. It is easier to shift the rear derailleur after you are into the climb than the front derailleur.

Okay. Now look at the trail and pick a route that will miss most of the visible rocks and roots. Note any loose rocks and rocks covered by soil. As you power into the climb, remember your old high school physics class, where you learned that momentum equals mass times velocity. Momentum is very important, and because your mass will stay fairly constant, your velocity is the key. Try to increase your velocity and pedal using your whole crank, pulling across the bottom and pushing across the top, and not just pounding down on the pedals, for this will break traction and compromise progress.

As the grade steepens, stay in the saddle as long as you can but without putting too much weight on it, because as you bump over rocks, you don't want to be bouncing onto the saddle. Maintain a balance between keeping enough weight on the saddle to maintain traction, and moving your shoulders forward to keep the front wheel on the ground. A good spin will keep you going straight and on your chosen route, but letting the front wheel rise too much and pressing the pedal with one foot or the other will force the front wheel to move back and forth, causing you to lose balance. As the grade gets steeper still, grab your climbing bars and shift your whole weight farther forward until you are completely out of the saddle. As you do this, pull back on the bars, forcing the rear wheel onto the ground.

One of the toughest obstacles on technical climbs is rocks and slick roots, which your rear wheel has to get over without slipping and spinning out. This is where you need that momentum you brought into the climb. When you see a root or rock that is going to compromise traction, plan for it. Power into it, building momentum, and pull your front wheel up over it. Then, as your rear wheel reaches the obstruction, let up and lean forward, pulling the rear wheel up over it with your feet and pedals. As soon as your wheel has cleared the root or rock, begin pedaling hard to get your speed back up for the next obstruction.

In the unfortunate event that obstructions are not spaced far enough apart so that you can plan from one to the next, take this opportunity to really test your skill. There are stretches at White Ranch and other parks where you have to get the front wheel over a water-diversion log as the back wheel is clearing one. There are many trails where your rear wheel is pushing through rocks as you guide your front wheel through the next rock or root. In these cases, the only answer is to power through while trying to shift your weight, keep traction with your rear wheel, lift the front wheel, and keep your balance as your speed drops off. This is a common scenario for losing traction, causing your pedals to spin momentarily. A painful result could be your knee hitting the handlebars, or you could topple over.

As you negotiate rocks and roots, plan for where your rear wheel is going to trace. Your front wheel can roll over obstructions with little trouble, but your weight and power are going to the rear, so use your balance and strength to keep your rear wheel on line and crank up the slope.

Downhills—What Is and What Never Should Be

Many descents on trails are not horribly steep, so braking and choosing a route through rocks and roots isn't a problem. There are, however, nearly as many cases in which braking has to be done while dropping over steep rocky slopes or into creekbeds. In these cases, your momentum is not your friend but must be controlled by proper braking.

Just as you do when approaching a steep climb, set up for a technical descent by carefully surveying the trail and picking a route through the rocks. And, just as with climbing, think in terms of your rear wheel when descending. In this case, though, you want to put your center of gravity over your rear wheel and extend your arms, gripping your handlebars and brake levers. Better control is obtained by using one or two of the middle fingers to brake while gripping the handlebars firmly. Braking on descents goes contrary to how most people approach cycling, and that is because of a fear of the front brake lever. If your bike fits you and you have good technique with your butt way out behind your saddle, it is nearly impossible to do an *endo* by braking too hard with the front brake.

There is no worse damage done to a trail than when cyclists ride down grades dragging their rear wheels in full skid. Once you *are* skidding, braking the rear wheel does little to reduce your speed and certainly doesn't improve your control. Keep both the front and rear brakes on before entering a technical stretch to reduce your speed *before* getting into it. Brake with your rear wheel as much as possible, but let up if you feel it start to skid. There are rare times when even the front wheel may skid a little bit if you are going too fast, but this will quickly stop, either because you have decelerated, or because you have crashed. Again, applying the brakes to both wheels is the most effective way to slow down. And even more important is controlling your speed by using your brakes while you are on parts of the trail where they will be most effective—*before* the most technical sections. If you see skid marks heading off into the woods or approaching a trail junction, then you will see where others should have controlled their speed before they got there.

Braking the front wheel does have its disadvantages, such as in very rough sections of trail. If there is a big rock or dip (for example, a gully or water-diversion log) coming up that looks like it could jam your front wheel, release the front brake just as you reach it while pulling up on your handlebars, allowing the wheel to roll over the obstruction. Resume braking after your front tire has rolled over the obstruction. When there are several rocks or logs in sequence, you may end up braking and releasing in repetition. At this point, keep your weight back over the rear wheel and use your balance, taking advantage of gravity to keep you going and the equilibrium of braking and rolling to get the front tire over obstacles.

Another place on descents where speed can become a problem is when you encounter a water-diversion structure. A water-diversion structure can be ditches dug across the trail or old four-wheel-drive roads to divert runoff off to the side; a log or other object half-buried and lying across the trail; or soil pushed up into a berm crossing the trail, creating a water bar. Water bars can be as high as a couple of feet. One thing that one should never attempt is to *get air* off a water-diversion structure when riding down a steep incline. The physics of the situation are this: You are moving downhill at a good fetch and you come to a water bar. Your front wheel is propelled upward by the ramp, and you think, "I'm really going to get some air on this one!" But because you are on an incline, your front wheel dives as your rear wheel is propelled upward by the ramp.

Your body's speed overtakes that of your bike, you see the ground coming, and you think, "I'm going to die!" You find yourself, we hope, sprawled on the trail with only a few scratches, but your front wheel is in the shape of a taco as your heart-rate monitor beeps madly. And finally, you find that, contrary to the tee-shirt slogan, chicks don't really dig mountain biking scars.

If you are new to technical descents, it is a good idea to avoid trying to ride them until you are ready for them. If you get into one that is over your head, don't try to bail out by dropping off your saddle and straddling the top tube (the bar on your frame that connects the seat to the steering tube). On a steep grade this will shift your weight too far forward and you are likely to topple over the handlebars headfirst. Instead, slow yourself as much as possible and keep your balance while keeping your butt behind the saddle. When you have come to a nearly complete stop, place your foot on a rock or the uphill side of the trail and get off the bike while holding the brakes firmly. Never let your weight get too far forward. Get your bike adjusted to fit you, get a good feel for it, and develop confidence in addressing tough downhills.

To reiterate, speed on downhills, when it gets away from you, combines with your mass to build momentum that is very hard to reduce when you are on really rough terrain. Your wheels start to skip and bounce and you will almost certainly lose control. Blind curves and associated hikers, cyclists, horses, and other obstacles can also come up very quickly. So do everyone a favor and control your speed, and help keep Colorado trails open to mountain bikes.

HOW TO USE THIS BOOK

*R*ides in this book are organized along major thoroughfares or by towns proximal to Denver. The major north-south transportation routes used in this book are Interstate 25 and the smaller roads along the foothills, including state highway (SH) 93 and U.S. highway 36. The two major thoroughfares to the Front Range from Denver proper are Interstate 70 and U.S. highway 285 (Hampden Avenue in Littleton and Englewood). Both of these routes lead to a number of trails and are easy to find from Denver, Boulder, Fort Collins, and other Front Range cities. Other routes that are not major thoroughfares but connect to several trails are SH 14, which runs along the Poudre River from Fort Collins to North Park; the Peak to Peak Highway (SH 72 and SH 119), which connects Nederland to Estes Park; SH 93 and US 36, which traverse the foot of the range between Golden and Lyons and on northward to Estes Park; and the numerous state highways that travel up area canyons.

Towns that are located near a number of trails—Fort Collins, Boulder, Golden, Idaho Springs, and Evergreen—are used for locating groups of trails. These towns may be good places to stay if you are visiting the state, because several trails can be accessed from any of them.

This book is unique in that its maps are digital images of the rides, so that you can get a feel for the terrain on which you will be riding. This is done by using digital elevation-model data that is available on the Internet from the U.S. Geological Survey (USGS). Data was also digitized from topographic maps when the detail of the USGS data was not sufficient. Trails were mapped either from existing park maps or from Forest Service or USGS maps and then were many times updated in the field. The specific USGS 7 1/2-minute quadrangle maps that cover each ride or group of rides are listed at the beginning of each ride description. Maps, even after incorporating high-tech data and computer imaging, are still approximate, and distances can vary on your individual bike computer. Many of the parks in the Front Range are new and are being changed by the local counties, cities, or the state park system, typically by having added to them new acreage and trails (e.g., Rabbit Mountain Park). Trails are also always changing with respect to their usage restrictions, and some that were not mentioned in this book may now be open to mountain bikes, whereas some that are now open may be closed in the future. Consult USGS topographic maps and maps available at trailheads and local ranger stations for additional access information.

The Front Range butts right up against the Great Plains, and although Denver, Boulder, and the other cities in the area are within sight of the Front Range, they are actually located on the Great Plains, just as Salina, Kansas, is. The difference is that the drive to get to the huge uplifted block called the central Rocky Mountains is much shorter for folks in Denver than for those in Salina.

Though we made an effort to find easy as well as hard rides, the trails described in this book are, for the most part, mountain bike rides that require a good deal of fitness at both moderate and high altitudes, some as high as 12,000 feet. Most of the rides are far below this elevation. If you are venturing up one of the rides that will climb over 10,000 feet, it is a good idea to have a number of rides under your belt at a 5,000- to 8,000-foot elevation.

Some of the rides are fairly technical (large rocks and steep grades) and are not suitable for cyclists with low-end equipment or limited experience. Because of this, the rides are rated as easy, moderate, or difficult, based on the grade, distance, and the technical nature of the trail or road. Easy rides are a combination of fairly smooth trail or road, low grades, and short distances (less than, say, 10 miles). If a ride is exceptionally flat, it may still be rated easy or easy to moderate, even though it may be longer. Moderate rides are either short and somewhat technical, or over 15 miles and not technical with gradual grades. Difficult trails are technical, long, include significant climbs, or have all these elements. There are, obviously, a great number of factors that go into rating a trail, and we try to explain why each trail is rated the way it is. Our goal is to provide a rating based on the effort and skill required by the average cyclist in order to finish the ride.

There are a variety of rides, so cyclists of all skill levels should be able to find at least a few rides, and many of the routes can be shortened or lengthened to make them easier or harder to suit your preference. There are a couple of routes that are easy and could be fun for the whole family, or as a good rehabilitation ride after ski season and the associated orthopedic repair procedures.

The rides are listed in regional order from north to south and correspond to the location map on page ii. Each ride is mapped with pertinent features and roads and, along with elevation contours, is overlain on a digital elevation model of the terrain. Judge the ride difficulty by looking at how many contours the trail crosses, and use the 3-D perspective of the model to get a feel for how much climbing and descending is involved.

If you are not familiar with some of the cycling terminology used in this book, refer to the glossary beginning on page 189. Slang words that appear in the glossary are in italics in the text. We must note, however, that slang terms change quickly, so don't be too upset if some of the terms appear antiquated.

Many of the trails described herein were ridden on a solid mountain bike with no suspension fork or rear suspension. The bike weighed around thirty pounds, which, you may note, is quite heavy according to today's standards. It did, however, have top-of-the-line components and wheels—albeit from 1993. Other trails—at least half of them—were ridden with a more up-to-date high-end mountain bike with a suspension fork, but every effort was made to take into consideration the lower-end bikes that many people are riding. So, the trails are rated as most people will experience them. If you are experienced or are into *gonzo-abusive* radical rides or both, you may find the descriptions and ratings in this book quite conservative and cautious. Even so, we promote common sense on every ride.

Remember the rules of the trail, which include traveling at a controllable speed and yielding to horses, hikers, and wildlife. Dogs should yield to all of the above, so be cautious around them and control your own pet. As the population of the Denver metro area grows every year, forest and trail users also grow in number, and the best way to keep trails open to bicycles is to be courteous when riding and not to damage the trails by skidding your tires. The congestion issue can be made easier by scheduling rides during off-peak hours or days, some of which are noted in the text for each ride.

So tune up your bike and head for the hills, and *always* wear your helmet!

FORT COLLINS
area

*F*ort Collins is located about an hour north of Denver on Interstate 25 (I-25) and is at the mouth of the Cache la Poudre River, referred to locally as the Poudre River. French trappers named the river *Cache la Poudre* for the gunpowder they stored there for future use by mountain men. The headwaters of the Poudre River are near the east side of Cameron Pass, and on the west side lies North Park. This area is rich in wildlife, including elk, deer, bear, and moose and includes some gold medal trout streams.

Fort Collins, like all of the "fort" towns in the West, is named after a military establishment. Camp Collins, named after Colonel W. O. Collins of Fort Laramie (don't ask us why that fort is now called simply "Laramie" and Fort Collins isn't called "Camp Collins"), was maintained in the 1860s to protect the overland mail line from hostile Native Americans in the area. The mail line ran between Denver and Laramie, Wyoming, along the route now traversed by I-25. The mail was later carried by the railroad, and in 1872 the camp was disbanded. It wasn't really needed anyway, because the U.S. Army controlled the area by that time. A Frenchman named Antoine Janis, who called the town Colona, had founded the nearby town of Laporte earlier, in 1844. It is not known whether he rode a Janis mountain bike.

Fort Collins later became an agricultural settlement that grew, overtaking Laporte, the original Larimer County seat, as a trading and political center. Fort Collins is now the home of Colorado State University, a leading engineering, veterinary science, natural resources, and agricultural school, among other fields.

Rides west of Fort Collins are some of the best in the state's Front Range and explore some beautiful forests and historic mining areas.

Seven Mile Creek Loop

Rating: Moderate to difficult

Distance: 13 miles round-trip

Time required: 2–4 hours

Notes: Tough climb—not real steep but lots of loose angular cobbles; creek crossings; easy descent on improved roads

Quadrangles: South Ball Mtn., Rustic, Red Feather Lakes, Kinikinik

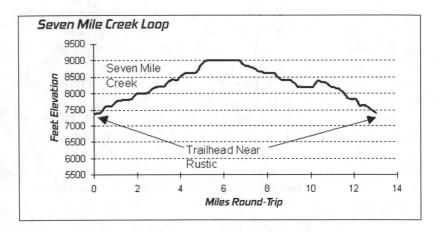

The small enclave of Rustic is located up the Poudre Canyon west from Fort Collins on SH 14, 31 miles west of the junction of SH 14 and US 287. Rustic is a good jumping-off point for a number of challenging rides, including the Seven Mile Creek ride. Turn right (north) on County Road (CR) 69, which leads to Pingree Hill just as you come upon Rustic, and proceed for about a quarter of a mile on the dirt road to an unmarked turnoff that goes to the left. Park at the wide area on the right.

This ride is a loop that takes you up the rough and strenuous Seven Mile Creek road through historic mining country, then across the top of the uplands and back down improved roads. This ride can easily be extended to fit your ability or desired level of exertion, or

Seven Mile Creek Loop

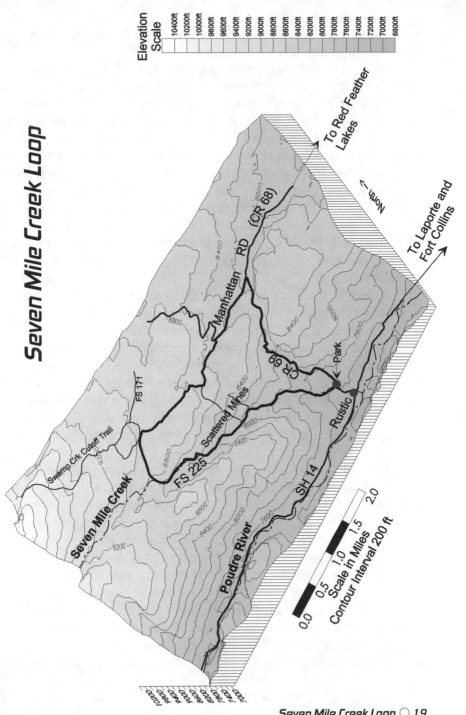

Elevation Scale

10400ft
10200ft
10000ft
9800ft
9600ft
9400ft
9200ft
9000ft
8800ft
8600ft
8400ft
8200ft
8000ft
7800ft
7600ft
7400ft
7200ft
7000ft
6800ft

To Red Feather Lakes

North

To Laporte and Fort Collins

Manhattan Rd (CR 68)

FS 171

Swamp Crk Cutoff Trail

Seven Mile Creek

Scattered Mines

FS 225

CR 69

Park

Rustic

SH 14

Poudre River

0.0   0.5   1.0   1.5   2.0
Scale in Miles
Contour Interval 200 ft

you can ride it backwards—not literally, of course, but do the climbing part on the smoother CR 69 to make it easier.

From the parking area, ride up the rough four-wheel-drive road, Forest Service (FS) 225, up Seven Mile Creek past many campsites and watching for out-of-control ATVs (all-terrain vehicles) and motorcycles. The first 4 miles is a tiring romp over rocky terrain and through at least three creek crossings, one deep enough to submerge your bottom bracket. Between cranking over rocks, some of which are loose, there are patches of coarse sand that will also sap your energy. Try to avoid the sand and look for a smooth path through the rocks. At 4 miles there is a small park and a fork in the road. Bear right (north), because the left fork heads to the Roaring Creek Trail and SH 14. Climb past the ruins of a mine and small boardinghouse as the road gets a bit smoother and climbs in earnest to the north.

A little past 5 miles out you will reach another junction, with two roads that lead off to the northwest and one that leads off to the northeast (your right). Bear right on the northeast fork and rejoice, because you have just about finished climbing. If you feel like you want to ride some more, head left instead on what is essentially the middle fork to explore some more mine ruins, or ride all the way up the Swamp Creek trail (FS Trail 871) to FS 517, which will bring you back down Elkhorn Creek (note that elk don't have horns, they have antlers) to CR 162. This will add about 15 tough miles to the original 13-mile loop.

If you didn't head left at the junction, continue on the return route until, at about 7.5 miles, you hit the main road, CR 162 (not shown on our map). Turn right and drop rapidly in elevation past the Manhattan town site, and at about 9 miles you'll come to the junction with CR 69 where you turn right (south). This junction is not well marked (the sign is small and low to the ground) with regard to its connection with SH 14, so watch for it; if you miss this turn you will never be heard from again. Well, it won't be that bad, but you will drop more in elevation and there is no other connection with SH 14 till you get to Livermore. Don't miss this turn onto CR 69.

After climbing on CR 69 for about a mile up one last hill, there is nothing but descending on the improved gravel road for the

A rider making his way up the Seven Mile Creek Climb.

remaining 3 miles to your car. There are a number of other roads and trails in this area that good maps will show. If you want to make life harder, pick another route to add to this one. Conversely, if you are not ready for a climb such as that along Seven Mile Creek, drive on up CR 69 to CR 162 and ride the roads at the top. These roads are not as technical and don't climb nearly as much.

Hewlett Gulch Trail

Rating: Moderate to difficult

Distance: 10 miles round-trip as described

Time required: 2–3 hours

Notes: Technical spots; tough climbs; creek crossings; wide variety of terrain; a fun ride and good workout

Quadrangles: Poudre Park, Livermore Mountain

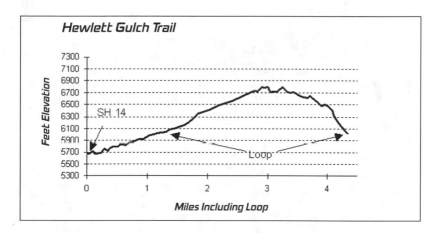

This ride is a single track with many shallow creek crossings and alternating smooth and technical stretches. There are a couple of good climbs, one being an impossible steep and technical wall climb (if you can ride it let us know), and the other a long, gradual climb on a smooth single track. There is also an unrideable (at least for the sane) downhill and a variety of terrain and scenery.

Only 9 miles west from the junction of US 287 and SH 14 in Fort Collins, and just past the enclave of Poudre Park, maybe a mile, is the Poudre Park Picnic Area. Between Poudre Park and the Poudre Park Picnic Area is the turnoff to Hewlett Gulch, a popular mountain bike ride. There is limited parking along SH 14 near the bridge that crosses the Cache la Poudre River. It is easier and safer to park at

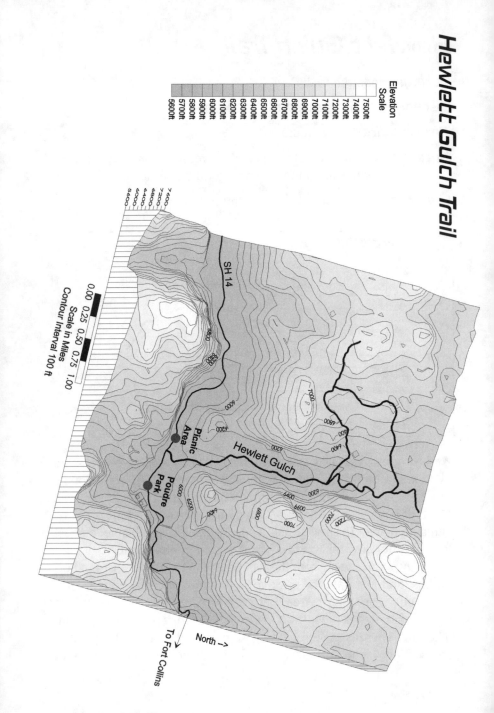

Elevation
Scale

7500ft
7400ft
7300ft
7200ft
7100ft
7000ft
6900ft
6800ft
6700ft
6600ft
6500ft
6400ft
6300ft
6200ft
6100ft
6000ft
5900ft
5800ft
5700ft
5600ft

SH 14

Picnic
Area

Poudre
Park

Hewlett Gulch

0.00 0.25 0.50 0.75 1.00
Scale in Miles
Contour Interval 100 ft

North ->

To Fort Collins

the picnic area and ride east to the bridge and dirt road that leads to the trail.

Head across the bridge over the Poudre River and follow the unmarked dirt road for a quarter of a mile to where the trail leaves the road to the left (north). A private residence is on the right. From here the trail follows the creek that runs in Hewlett Gulch, passing the remnants of old houses and crossing the creek at least ten times in the first 3 miles (we lost count).

The well-used single-track trail winds north up the narrow canyon, crossing sandy and smooth point-bar areas covered by sediment washed down from the hillsides and deposited by the creek during periodic small rainfall runoffs. Leaving the point bars and crossing the creek, the trail then drops into the active creek channel, which is exposing boulders and cobbles washed down during huge rainfall events and the resulting flash floods. This combination of sandy point bars and rocky creek channel makes each creek crossing technical as you go in and out. The channel bottom, however, is smooth, because it is covered with sand currently being moved along by the water that you will be riding through.

There are a couple of places in the first few miles where trail use has exposed roots, so watch out for them. At about 2.5 miles a trail takes off to the left (west). Continue straight on, because this second trail is unrideable.

Schist happens. Schist is a metamorphic rock that is so changed by heat and pressure while buried deep within the earth's crust that all its minerals have been rotated and separated, and many have been altered to mica and hornblende. Schist looks almost silky at first glance (phylite is a very silky silvery gray rock that is similar to both schist and slate) and has well-developed foliation, or layers of different minerals. (There is also gneiss in the area, a rock with good foliation but not the silky sheen.) Schist is important to you because it is what the trail crosses at 3.25 miles as its course leaves the confines of Hewlett Gulch and climbs onto the uplands. Here is a several hundred foot climb that begins on a lot of rubble then moves onto schist that is weathering quickly and does not afford much traction. You may notice that the silky sheen of the schist, which is caused by the mica, makes its surface slick. Also notice

One of many stream crossings along the Hewlett Gulch Trail.

that it weathers more than other rocks, producing more rubble and sand, which are problems on steep climbs.

After carrying your bike up the aforementioned climb, follow the trail on up and across the grassy upland surfaces. Ride the single track across the meadows to where it drops and then climbs through a series of ups and downs. At about the 5.5-mile point the trail splits. Bear left unless you want to ride a couple of miles of undulating trail out to a dead end for a side trip.

There is about a half-mile downhill stretch just before the 6-mile point where the trail drops back into Hewlett Gulch that we do not recommend for riding. The trail looks like it was cut by a bulldozer driven down the ridge for a firebreak, after which nature was left to run its course, which, of course produced rubble and rotten metamorphic rocks. You will probably have to walk down this stretch. After a little more than 6 rough miles, you are back on the trail at the junction previously noted at 2.5 miles from the dirt road. There are only a few creek crossings between you and SH 14.

There are other possible ride combinations on this route that could make it a bit more of a workout, but don't be fooled by the short distance of 10 miles. This is a good workout and a good place to work on several different mountain bike skills.

Flowers Road/Monument Gulch

Rating: Difficult

Distance: 32 miles round-trip

Time required: 4–6 hours

Notes: This ride is on four-wheel-drive and improved dirt roads, is very long, and gains a lot of elevation between 6,000 and 9,000 feet in altitude

Quadrangles: Pingree Park, Crystal Mountain, Buckhorn Mountain

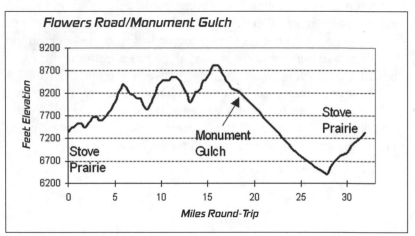

Flowers Road/Monument Gulch

*L*ocated just northeast of Rocky Mountain National Park and west of Lory State Park, Flowers Road (FS 152) is not only a good ride in its own right but provides access to several other possibilities on the four-wheel-drive roads in the area. This area can be explored using the Forest Service's Roosevelt National Forest map. The loop ride described follows four-wheel-drive roads through the forest at the foot of Rocky Mountain National Park. The ride is quite long, about 32 miles, but this area can be explored and shorter rides discovered.

To reach Flowers Road, take U.S. Highway 287 west from Fort Collins to the town of Laporte. In Laporte, turn left on to CR 54G, at

Flowers Road/Monument Gulch

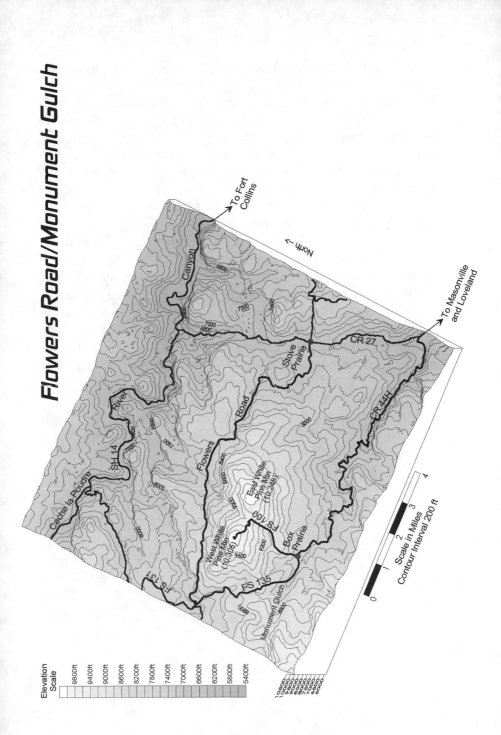

To Fort Collins

North →

To Masonville
and Loveland

Canyon

CR 27

Stove Prairie

CR 44H

River

SH 14

Flowers Road

Cache la Poudre

East White
Pine Mtn
(10,248ft)

West White
Pine Mtn
(10,305ft)

FS 100

Box Prairie

FS 135

FS 131

Monument Gulch

Elevation Scale

9800ft
9400ft
9000ft
8600ft
8200ft
7800ft
7400ft
7000ft
6600ft
6200ft
5800ft
5400ft

Scale in Miles
0 1 2 3 4
Contour Interval: 200 ft

the sign for Rist Canyon. Take CR 54G for about 2.5 miles to a cross-roads named Bellvue and keep going straight ahead, now on CR 52E. This road, known as the Rist Canyon Road, winds around and climbs into the Front Range for about 13 miles to a crossroads known as Stove Prairie. Stove Prairie can also be reached by driving west along the Poudre River on SH 14 from Laporte, northwest of Fort Collins. The turnoff (onto CR 27) for Stove Prairie is about 5 miles past Poudre Park and 1.5 miles west of Mishawaka. Head south on CR 27 for about 9 miles to Stove Prairie. Stove Prairie itself consists of a 4-way intersection, a school house, and rows of mailboxes.

Park along the road at the Stove Prairie crossroads and ride west on Flowers Road, the continuation of CR 52E to the west. This climb is fairly gradual, but significant elevation (a total of about 1,000 feet) is gained over the 14 miles to the first turn at FS 135.

After you turn left (south) on FS 135, the road climbs up a draw, gaining 800 feet of elevation in 2.5 miles before dropping down into Monument Gulch. This is the last climb for quite a while, for you now ride down the Box Prairie Creek Road (CR 44H) for 15 miles. This stretch of road is in the Buckhorn Creek canyon and is down-hill all the way to Road 27, a total drop of about 1,600 feet.

From Box Prairie, you can take a side trip north and west and climb up to the top of West White Pine Mountain (10,305 feet in ele-vation). This ride goes up an old four-wheel-drive road and climbs about 2,000 feet in just under 3 miles. This might be a bit much if you are doing the whole loop.

When you reach Road 27 turn left (north) and begin the final leg and climb of the ride back to Stove Prairie. This leg is about 5 miles and climbs exactly 910 feet.

There is some motor vehicle traffic on this loop, including four-wheel-drives and motorcycles, though not enough to make it dan-gerous. This area is popular during hunting season, so be careful during the late fall.

Lory State Park and Horsetooth Mountain Park

Rating: Variable depending on route chosen—easy to very difficult; trail ratings described independently

Distance: 20 miles for the loop, other rides vary

Time required: 3–6 hours

Notes: Very rocky trail, good climbs with technical climbs and descents; can be very warm in the summer. Fee area—$3/car, $2/bicycle or walk-in

Quadrangles: Horsetooth Reservoir

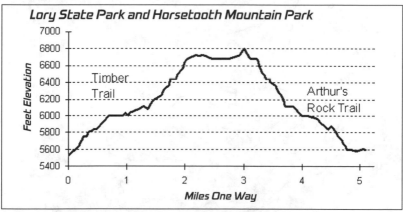

Lory State Park and Horsetooth Mountain Park

Feet Elevation / *Miles One Way*

Timber Trail

Arthur's Rock Trail

(Note: elevation profile shows the route's major climb and descent only; it does not show entire ride.)

Lory State Park and adjoining Horsetooth Mountain Park offer virtually every level of ride, including smooth rolling trails through grassy fields, steep long climbs, and many technical ascents and descents. The parks contain picnic areas, backcountry camping, several foot-only trails, and over 25 miles of mountain bike trails. Lory State Park was purchased by the state of Colorado from local ranchers in 1967 and named in honor of Colorado State University's president from 1909 to 1940, Dr. Charles A. Lory (1872–1969).

Horsetooth Reservoir is located just west of Fort Collins and was created by the construction of earthen dams in water gaps,

Lory State Park and Horsetooth Mountain Park

Trails: (heavy lines)
1 Soderberg
2 Horsetooth Rock
3 Horsetooth Falls
4 Waithen
5 Spring Creek
6 Westridge (in Horsetooth)
7 Stout
8 Sawmill
9 East Ridge
10 Mill Creek
11 Loggers
12 Arthur's Rock
13 Timber
14 Westridge (in Lory)
15 Valley Trail
Foot-only trails not shown
TGPA: Timber Group Picnic Area

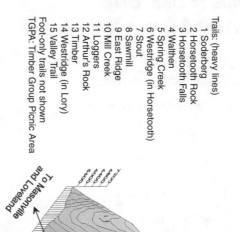

Contour Interval 100 ft.
Scale in Miles
0.0 0.5 1.0 1.5 2.0

To Masonville
and Loveland

Horsetooth
Mtn Park
Entrance

Horsetooth Pk Bndry

Lory S.P. Bndry

Horsetooth
Lory S.P.
Entrance

TGPA

Horsetooth Reservoir

To Fort Collins

CR 38E

CR 25

CR 28E

CR 38E

CR 25G

North →

To Fort Collins

Elevation
Scale
5000ft
5100ft
5200ft
5300ft
5400ft
5500ft
5600ft
5700ft
5800ft
5900ft
6000ft
6100ft
6200ft
6300ft
6400ft
6500ft
6600ft
6700ft
6800ft
6900ft
7000ft
7100ft
7200ft

where creeks draining the Front Range have cut through hogbacks of uplifted and tilted sedimentary rocks. Thus, the reservoir is a long, narrow, north-south trending body of water with Front Range igneous and metamorphic rocks on the west and steeply dipping sedimentary rocks on the east. Roads around the east side of Horsetooth Mountain Park provide additional riding through some very rugged foothill country.

Varied wildlife and plant species are present within both parks. The lower valley along Horsetooth Reservoir consists of grassy rolling meadows. The more arid lower hillsides, particularly the south-facing ones, are home to many lizard species, rattlesnakes, yucca, prickly pear cactus (did you bring a patch kit?), and numerous shrubs. The wetter hillsides (higher and north-facing) support ponderosa forest. Throughout the parks, animals such as mule deer, mountain lion, black bear, coyote, Abert's squirrel, cottontail rabbit, blue grouse, mourning dove, wild turkey, and many songbirds may be seen. Checklists of bird and plant species may be obtained at each park's entrance station. Horsetooth Reservoir is one of the few places in the area where eagles nest.

To reach Lory State Park or Horsetooth Mountain Park from Denver, follow I-25 north toward Fort Collins. Take the Prospect Road exit to Fort Collins and turn left (west). Take Prospect past Fort Collins to Overland Trail Road and turn right (north) on Overland Trail. After several miles, a sign at Bingham Hill Road (CR 50E) will designate Lory State Park. Turn Left on Bingham Hill Road. Go up and over Bingham Hill and turn left (south) on CR 23N. Follow this road until the dam to Horsetooth Reservoir looms above and the sign to Lory State Park beckons you to turn right on CR 25G. Do so, and enter the park. There is a $3 per-car fee and a $2 fee for bicycle/walk-in entry. Note the water spigot before the park entrance on the left side of the road.

Horsetooth Mountain Park is located south of Lory State Park, so, to reach it, continue south on CR 25G, climbing past the dam. This road will skirt the east side of Horsetooth Reservoir for about 7 miles, crossing two more dams and affording some views of the plains, Fort Collins, and Hughes Stadium, where Colorado State University holds football games. At about 5 miles from the turnoff to Lory State Park, and just after crossing the second dam, the road tees into CR 38E. Bear right and continue south. About two miles after the road wraps around the south end of the reservoir, the entrance to Horsetooth Mountain Park will come up on the right (north) side.

An alternative route to the parks from Boulder is to head north on SH 119 for 12 miles to Longmont, following the signs to Loveland through the downtown area. Turn left (north) on US 287 and drive 12 miles to the small town of Berthoud. Continue on through Berthoud for 7 miles to Loveland. Continue north for another 8 miles to SH 68, also named Harmony Road. Take a left (west) on Harmony Road, where in 2 miles it will tee into Taft Hill Road. Take a right (north) and drive for only one half mile to CR 38E, which takes off to the left and winds up the hills toward Horsetooth Reservoir. County Route 38E intersects CR 23 when you reach the reservoir, but bear left (south), staying on CR 38E, and follow it around the south end of the reservoir for about 4 miles to the entrance to Horsetooth Mountain Park, which will be on the right (north).

The three looping trails described here can be ridden in any number of combinations of varying difficulty in both Lory and Horsetooth Mountain parks. For all of these loops, enter Lory State Park from the north and take the first right into the Timber Group Picnic Area and park there (elevation 5,550 feet).

Valley Trail Loop: Easy; 10 miles round-trip

This is an easy ride through the valley on the east side of Lory State Park. There are other side trails that lead to the reservoir's edge and make connections to trails that lead up into the hills. This loop goes south on the west side of the main park access road and returns on the east side.

To ride the loop, take the Timber Trail from the left side of the parking lot. After a short distance the trail forks, with the Valley Trail veering left and Timber Trail veering right. *Stay to the left!* The Valley Trail parallels the main park access road (the only road in the park) on the east side through the park and crosses the foot-only Well Gulch Nature Trail. At 3 miles the trail intersects the road at a parking and turn-around area. The Shoreline Trail to the east of the parking area is an optional 1-mile spur (a short dead-end trail) that leads to the edge of Horsetooth Reservoir (2 miles round trip).

Continue south on the Valley Trail out of the parking area and onto the rolling meadows. The trail drops down off a hill and dips through small sand-bottomed ravines until it ends at a service road at mile 5, 2 miles from the last parking area. Turn around at this point and head back to that parking area. From the parking area, head right (east) on the Shoreline Trail. Take the Shoreline Trail for less than half a mile to the first left. Take this left and follow the eastern branch of the Valley Trail, which follows the main access road back to the Timber Group Picnic Area. An alternative to the Valley Trail is the main road through the park.

Timber Trail/Arthur's Rock Trail Loop: Difficult; 8.5 miles round-trip, technical climbs and descents

From the Timber Group Picnic Area, take the Timber Trail out of the left side of the parking lot. Stay right past the fork with the Valley Trail that heads left. The Timber Trail immediately begins to climb through some steep switchbacks. The trail is a very narrow and rocky single track with cactus and brush on either side through much of the climb. The trail continues to climb steeply up switchbacks until it joins the Westridge Trail. Stay to the right on Timber Trail. The trail levels off and continues through pine forest, passes backcountry campsites, and finally reaches Arthur's Rock after 3.5 brutal miles and 1,200 feet of elevation gain. The good news is that this is the highest point on the trail.

The trail now becomes the Arthur's Rock Trail. Continue, descending on Arthur's Rock Trail, bearing right at upcoming forks and avoiding the Overlook Trail (foot only) and the foot-only portion of the Arthur's Rock Trail. Pass the Sawmill Trail, which comes in from the right, and switchback down into the meadow below as the trail turns north and intersects a parking area at 5.5 miles out. To get from here back to the Timber Group Picnic Area, where you began, you can either take the Valley Trail or the main access road (they parallel each other). Either way, it is 3 miles of easy riding back.

Lory State Park/Horsetooth Mountain Park Loop: Very difficult; 18.2 miles round-trip

This ride is a lengthy and tough collection of trails in both parks. It includes the route from the Timber Trail/Arthur's Rock Loop described above but also ventures south into Horsetooth Mountain Park. This ride could be considered a full-day affair, and your conditioning and bike should be at their best. There are a lot of rough trails, climbing, and descending, and good technique is required.

Following the route for the Timber Trail/Arthur's Rock Loop, take the Timber Trail out of the left side of the Timber Group Picnic Area parking lot. Bear right, staying on the Timber Trail past the left turn to the Valley Trail. Climb through some steep switchbacks on the narrow and rocky Timber Trail to where it joins the Westridge Trail. Continue to the right on Timber Trail as it levels off and leads through pine forest, passes backcountry campsites, and finally reaches Arthur's Rock after at the 3.5-mile mark.

On what is now the Arthur's Rock Trail, descend, bearing right at all upcoming forks and past the Sawmill Trail, which comes in from the right. The Timber Trail switchbacks down into the meadow below and to a parking area at the 5.5-mile point.

Continue south out of the parking area on the Sawmill Trail and onto the rolling meadows. The trail dips through small sand-bottomed ravines until it ends at an unnamed service road at 6.2 miles. Turn right on this rough and unimproved service road.

The service road climbs steeply for 3 miles to the microwave towers far above on Horsetooth Mountain. The trail from here on consists of loose rock and sand with technical ascents and descents. Most of the trail on the way down is not rideable and can be very hazardous. Be careful.

This section is very strenuous but intersects several trails that can be taken as bailouts back to the valley bottom. Stout Trail crosses the service road at 7.2 miles. This can be taken to the meadows below by turning right onto it and then taking another right onto Sawmill Trail. Similar bailouts can be taken on Loggers Trail at 7.6 miles, Herrington Trail at 7.9 miles, and Mill Creek Trail at 9 miles. If you're still cognizant at the Westridge Trail at 9.2 miles, turn right onto Westridge Trail.

The Westridge Trail, a single-track trail, climbs steeply for about a mile, with some technical descents mixed in, through ponderosa pine forest to the top of Horsetooth Mountain. At the summit, spectacular views of Horsetooth Mountain, the Great Plains, Horsetooth Reservoir, and the countryside to the west of Horsetooth Mountain Park abound.

At 10.6 miles, turn left onto Wathen Trail. Wathen Trail descends steep loose-rock hills and switchbacks into a grass-covered basin separated from the service road that you rode up on earlier by a small ridge. At 11.6 miles turn left on Spring Creek Trail, which climbs gradually to the junction with Herrington Trail at 11.7 miles. Turn right on the Herrington Trail and climb the short scramble past the junction with the Stout Trail that tees in from the right. Continue, bearing left on Herrington Trail back to the service road that will serve as the Herrington Trail temporarily.

Turn right on the service road and ride a short distance to the first left, which is the continuation of Herrington Trail. Take this left, and descend on Herrington Trail to the intersection with the Loggers Trail at 13.2 miles. Turn right on Loggers Trail and ride a short distance to Sawmill Trail. Turn right on Sawmill Trail and ride past Sawmill Cabin. Sawmill Trail descends steeply over loose rock and switchbacks to the valley below. Near the bottom of the mountain the trail veers north and intersects the Valley Trail at 14.2 miles. Turn left on Valley Trail here and ride the 4 rolling miles north back to the Timber Group Picnic Area. Remember that there is water at the Horsetooth Mountain Park entrance station.

ESTES PARK
area

*E*stes Park, unlike the East Coast trucking company, is pronounced as if it were spelled *Est-ess,* not *Estees.* The town of Estes Park is the original and busiest entrance to Rocky Mountain National Park and is situated at the head of the canyon of the Big Thompson River. Downstream from Estes Park is the site of the infamous and incredible flash flood of 1976 that killed some 150 people and virtually scoured the canyon of human structures. There was a similar though less destructive flood in Fort Collins in July of 1997 that caused millions of dollars in damage to homes and the Colorado State University bookstore and library.

The landscape around Estes Park was carved out of igneous and metamorphic rocks by glaciers that once covered the area to amazing depths. For more information on the glaciation of the area, visit the visitor center at Rocky Mountain National Park. Because Estes Park is the original entrance to Rocky Mountain National Park, it has the character of a Theodore Roosevelt–era mountain town and proudly features the majestic Stanley Hotel. This resort was the inspiration for Stephen King's novel and later movie *The Shining,* which has been filmed again for television using this hotel.

The Stanley Hotel was built by Paul Stanley of the rock group Kiss—not really. It was built by F. O. Stanley, the co-inventor of the Stanley Steamer, in 1909. He moved to the area in 1903 for health reasons and actually drove one of the Steamers to Estes Park from Boulder and later transported hotel guests up from Lyons with it on a regular basis.

Estes Park was named for Joel Estes, who in 1859 saw it as a place to live while he was bear hunting. It is not known if he killed any bears, but he did build a cabin and move his family into it. He left the area with his family in 1866 and moved to New Mexico, but the name stuck. In 1872 an Englishman, the earl of Dunraven, also on safari to Estes Park, liked the place and wanted to purchase it and start a housing development called Dunraven Ranches at Creekside. He was not permitted to do this, however, because he was a foreign national, but he did build the area's first hotel, the imaginatively named Estes Park Hotel, and a lake and peak in Rocky Mountain National Park are named after him, as well as a glade north of town. German-born artist Albert Bierstadt also frequented the area, painting the landscape. One of his paintings of Longs Peak once hung in the U.S. Capitol building.

Estes Park can be reached from Loveland through the canyon of the Big Thompson River via U.S. Highway 34 west, or by way of U.S. Highway 36 west from Lyons. There are plenty of places to eat in Estes Park, as well as outdoor-equipment dealers and mountain bike rental companies. Remember that the entrance fee for Rocky Mountain National Park is $5 per carload. The town is fairly congested with traffic throughout much of the May-through-August tourist season, but it's even more so when there are fall colors or rutting elk to view in Rocky Mountain National Park.

Crosier Mountain Trail

Rating: Difficult

Distance: 10.5 miles round-trip

Time required: 2–4 hours

Notes: Several good climbs, descents and rough trails

Quadrangles: Glen Haven, Drake

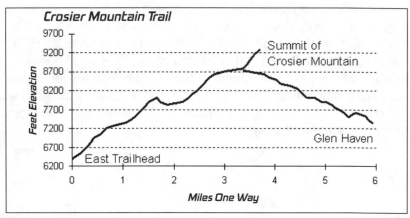

(Note: CR 43 connects ends; highway portion of ride not shown in elevation profile.)

This trail is a good example of rough Front Range single-track. There is a good amount of climbing and descending on the route and several good challenges to your technical riding ability. The Crosier Mountain Trail can be ridden as a loop or an up-and-back ride and can be started at four different trailheads. We will describe a loop ride going through two of the possible starting points.

To reach the Crosier Mountain area, drive north out of Estes Park on US 34 toward Fall River for one half mile past the Safeway store, then turn at the first right, CR 43, or Devil's Gulch Road. The first access point for Crosier Mountain Trail is at the southern side of Crosier Mountain. It is reached by continuing on CR 43 for 4 miles

Crosier Mountain Trail

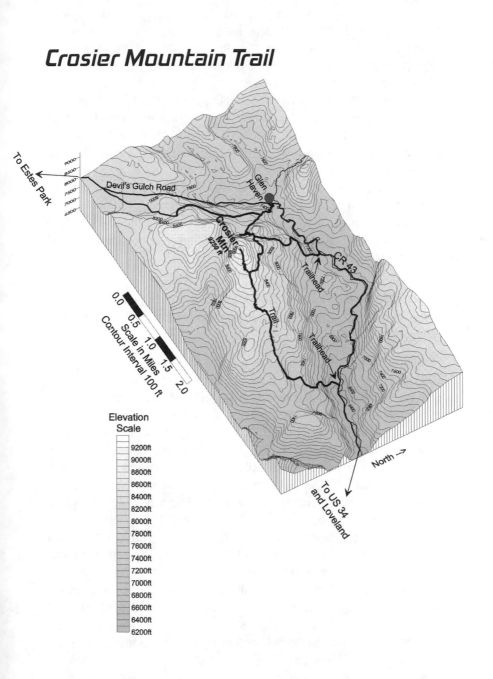

To Estes Park

Devil's Gulch Road

Glen Haven

Crosier Mtn. 9250 ft

CR 43

Trailhead

Trail

Trailhead

North →

To US 34 and Loveland

Scale in Miles
0.0 0.5 1.0 1.5 2.0
Contour Interval 100 ft

Elevation Scale

9200ft
9000ft
8800ft
8600ft
8400ft
8200ft
8000ft
7800ft
7600ft
7400ft
7200ft
7000ft
6800ft
6600ft
6400ft
6200ft

to a branch in the road, CR 61. Take a right (east) and look for parking along the gravel road. From here you could ride north on the road past a hostel and to the H-G Ranch trailhead. To lessen trail impact and increase convenience, it is recommended that you use one of the other trailheads.

To reach the next three trailheads, stay on SH 43 for 5 more miles to the enclave of Glen Haven, where the second trailhead (FS Trail 925) is on the right, 0.1-mile past the post office. There is no parking at the trailhead, so park at the intersection near the post office. The third trailhead (FS Trail 1013) is 2.2 miles from the post office, east of Glen Haven, past the Glen Haven and Lower North Fork Thompson picnic ground. The final trailhead (FS Trail 925) is about 7 miles past Glen Haven on the right side of the road. Both of the last two trailheads are marked with Forest Service signs, though you have to watch for the pullouts.

Crosier Mountain Loop: Difficult; 6.6 miles (10.2 miles with side trip) round-trip, difficult climbs and technical descents

Drive to the third Crosier Mountain trailhead, 2.2 miles east of Glen Haven just past the Lower North Fork Thompson picnic ground, as described above. The trail (FS Trail 1013) begins with an extremely steep climb southward out of the river valley. After 2 miles the trail begins to level somewhat. At 2.2 miles you will come to a junction. The left fork (FS Trail 925) is the Crosier Mountain Trail; it offers an optional 3.6-mile round-trip out-and-back spur to Crosier Mountain. The right fork drops past Piper Meadows and heads back to either Glen Haven or the H-G Ranch. Take the right to continue on the loop.

To ride the optional spur, take the left fork (Crosier Mountain Trail) and ride 1.8 miles east to the turnoff to the top of Crosier Mountain—ride or hike the short distance to the top. Turn around at this point and return to the trail, turning left (west) on Crosier Mountain Trail and returning to the junction with FS Trail 1013.

Continue on the loop riding straight ahead (west) on the right fork and drop down to Piper Meadows. At 2.7 total miles (6.3 miles

The Crosier Mountain Trailhead at the far east end.

if you took the side trip), on the southeast side of Piper Meadows the trail intersects the trail from the H-G Ranch that comes in from the left. Bear right and descend across the east side of Piper Meadows. Past the meadows the trail becomes steeper and more technical, with many exposed roots and increasingly large rocks. At 3.8 miles (7.4 miles with the side trip) the trail again intersects the H-G Ranch Trail (not shown on our map). Again, stay right on the Crosier Mountain Trail.

The trail now descends down very steep, narrow, and eroded switchbacks for 0.6-mile. Be cautious and aware of potentially heavy equestrian traffic, which has the right-of-way. At 4.4 miles the trail emerges among the houses of Glen Haven on a gravel road. Take the road on to CR 43 (Devil's Gulch Road). Turn right on CR 43, ride through Glen Haven, and descend the final 2.2 miles to the trailhead for 6.6 total miles—10.2 with the spur to the top of Crosier Mountain. County Road 43 is narrow and winding, with limited visibility, so ride near the edge of the road in single file and watch for automobile traffic.

Fall River Road
in Rocky Mountain National Park

Rating: Moderate

Distance: 30 miles (9 miles on dirt road, 21 miles on paved road) round-trip

Time required: 2–5 hours

Notes: A moderate climb but at high elevation; early start is recommended due to afternoon thunderstorms

Quadrangles: Fall River Pass, Trail Ridge

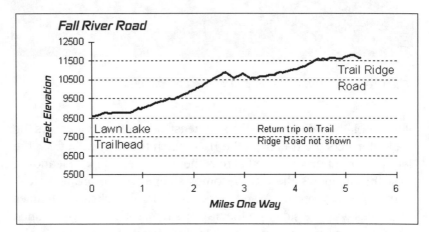

Fall River Road

Feet Elevation

Lawn Lake Trailhead

Trail Ridge Road

Return trip on Trail Ridge Road not shown

Miles One Way

Fall River Road is the original route through Rocky Mountain National Park. The road was constructed from 1913 to 1920 using the labor of thirty-eight inmates from the Colorado State Penitentiary. Trail Ridge Road, the current paved route through the park, was built to replace Fall River Road because of the latter's precipitous switchbacks and the difficulty of snow removal. Fall River Road is a hard-packed one-way (up) dirt road that is closed during the winter and most of the spring (typically from October through May) due to snowdrifts and avalanches. In the summer this ride provides an excellent workout and beautiful views of mountain canyons, Longs Peak, and surrounding mountains as it climbs

Fall River Road

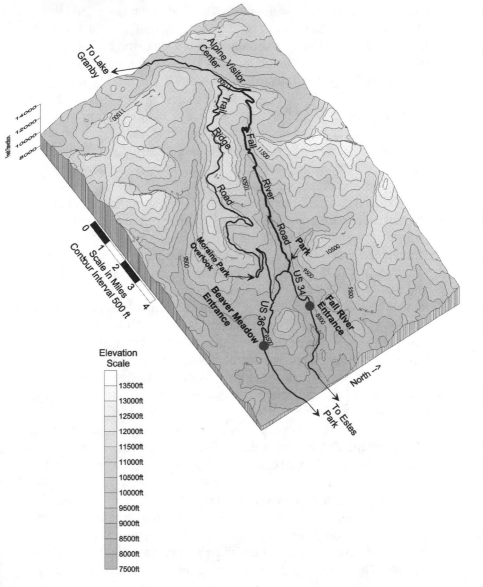

Elevation Scale

13500ft
13000ft
12500ft
12000ft
11500ft
11000ft
10500ft
10000ft
9500ft
9000ft
8500ft
8000ft
7500ft

through several different ecosystems, including riparian, montane, alpine, krummholz transition, and, finally, alpine tundra.

The trail is not technical to ride, consisting as it does of hard-packed sand with little loose rock, but with an elevation gain of 3,625 feet it is no cakewalk either. The ride down is on Trail Ridge Road, a narrow and winding paved road that can have heavy automobile traffic. Cars are not usually traveling fast, and cyclists do use the road regularly, but watch for cars entering the road from viewpoints, and for pedestrians in crosswalks.

The Fall River Road begins at 8,558 feet with a high point on Trail Ridge Road of 12,183 feet. Due to the high elevation and frequent and sudden afternoon thunderstorms that could include snow at any time of year, warm clothes and raingear should be packed. In early spring before the road is open to automobiles, snowslides and drifts and washed-out road sections may exist.

To reach Fall River Road, follow US 34 west out of Estes Park to the Fall River park entrance station. There is a $10 fee to enter the park. After a mile and a half, turn right on the road to Lawn Lake Trailhead. Continue for a quarter-mile and park at the parking lot.

Ride back to the Lawn Lake road and turn right. Ride 2 miles up and out of the broad glacial valley to the well-marked Fall River Road. The road turns to dirt and begins to climb through the montane ecosystem. This ecosystem consists of quaking aspen, lodgepole pine, ponderosa pine, and Douglas fir. Wildlife is also plentiful, including mule deer, elk, cottontail rabbit, coyote, bobcat, mountain lion, and the Abert's squirrel. A great variety of birds also live in this environment, including the great horned owl, northern goshawk, and broad-tailed hummingbird.

Reset your trip odometer, because the mileage from this point will reflect the distance from the beginning of the Fall River Road as reflected in the mile markers along the road. At 1.4 miles on the right are the 25-foot-high Chasm Falls. Through the next mile you may notice polished rocks and large boulders left behind by retreating glaciers as glacial drift. After 2 miles the transition to the alpine ecosystem is complete. The alpine ecosystem ranges from 9,000 feet in elevation to timberline, which is around 11,000 feet at this latitude. The alpine ecosystem is present for the next 6 miles to

The start of the climb up the old Fall River Road.

about mile 8. You may notice the following animals and plants as you gasp for breath in the ever-thinning air: pine marten, long-tailed weasel, red squirrel, snowshoe hare, elk, mule deer, porcupine, and coyote. Birds such as the Clark's nutcracker may be seen on branches of Englemann spruce, limber pine, Colorado blue spruce (the state tree), aspen, and lodgepole pine. If you don't see any wildlife, contact a park ranger and tell her that you paid full admission and expect to see something wild running or flying about.

The trail continues to climb through switchbacks. At mile 4 the 10,000-foot mark is passed. Rock spires can be seen to the upper right at mile 4.2. At 6.9 miles the Chapin Creek Trail is passed, along with the 11,000-foot mark. Over the next mile notice the trees becoming smaller and more twisted from the severe winter conditions. This is the krummholz (German for "crooked wood") zone, exemplified by the presence of low, twisted trees. From here through the alpine ecosystem birds such as the ptarmigan and animals such as the pika, marmot, Rocky Mountain bighorn sheep, and elk may be observed.

As you enter the tundra, all of the trees disappear, replaced by small shrubs, seasonal flowers, and clumps of grass that make up the tundra. Bare spots covered by sharp boulders interrupt the turf, pressed upward and tilted by water freezing in the soil. These patches are called "rock garlands" and "patterned ground" and provide habitat for the pika, a relative of the rabbit that will chirp at you as you walk or ride by. The vocal ones are actually warning others that a potential predator may be lurking in the area.

At 8.4 miles the road passes Chapin Creek Pass and the sewage treatment ponds for the Alpine Visitor Center, above. Finally, Fall River Pass (11,796 feet in elevation) is reached at mile 9, and just around the corner is the Alpine Visitor Center, snack bar, and gift shop, where food and collectors' travel spoons can be purchased. From here you will ride on Trail Ridge Road back to the Fall River Road and to your car. Incredulous tourists arriving by car will no doubt compliment you on your ride.

Ride through the parking lot and turn left (south) on the paved Trail Ridge Road. Climb the final 400 feet to the uppermost point of the ride (12,183 feet in elevation). The next 19 miles are full of excellent views of Longs Peak, herds of semi-tame elk, and some screaming descents. Trail Ridge Road is popular, and its traffic is typically heavy, so ride very carefully. Follow Trail Ridge Road all the way down, past the Moraine Park overlook and the beaver ponds in the glacial valley below and, finally, take a left at the intersection of US 34 and 36 and ride 1 mile back to the Lawn Lake trailhead.

Pole Hill Road

Rating: Difficult; hard climb and some technical sections

Distance: 6–10 miles round-trip

Time required: 1–3 hours

Notes: Short distance but strenuous climb

Quadrangles: Panorama Peak, Pinewood Lake

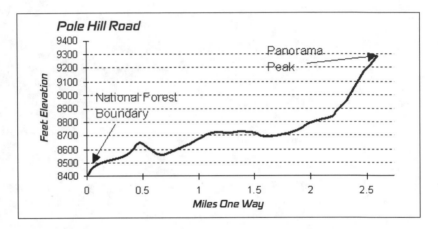

Pole Hill Road takes off to the east at the top of the last big hill before US 36 from Lyons drops into Estes Park. Turn east (right if coming from Lyons) off of highway 36 and drive on the gravel road (Pole Hill Road) that switchbacks through private land to the national forest boundary. If you really want some extra climbing, you can park at the Pole Hill Road turnoff in the cleared area to the west of US 36 and ride from there.

This ride features a series of climbs and level stretches that afford great views of the Front Range peaks to the west and the plains to the east. There are several climbs that are unbelievably steep, including the stretch to the summit of Panorama Peak, though the well-compacted rocks and clay soil provide surprisingly good traction.

Pole Hill Road

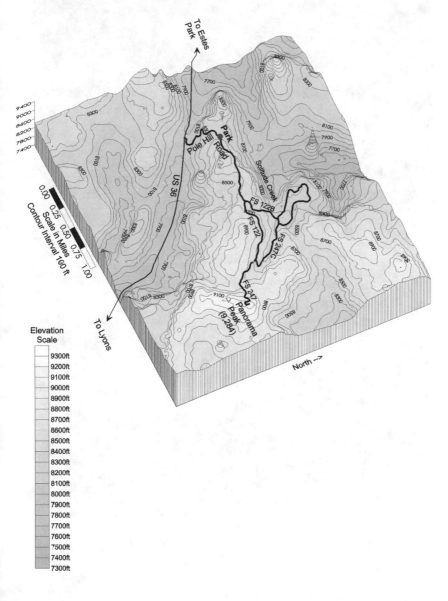

Elevation
Scale

9300ft
9200ft
9100ft
9000ft
8900ft
8800ft
8700ft
8600ft
8500ft
8400ft
8300ft
8200ft
8100ft
8000ft
7900ft
7800ft
7700ft
7600ft
7500ft
7400ft
7300ft

A lone rider pedals up a sun-drenched Pole Hill Road.

Drive or ride up Pole Hill Road through several switchbacks and past several driveways on the right to the Roosevelt National Forest boundary. There is a small parking area on the left here, or you can drive on for a bit and park along the road. It is good to go into this ride already a little bit warmed up, because you will start right off with a good climb. The ride as described begins on Pole Hill Road (FS 247), though you can take other combinations, such as FS 122B, which takes off to the left in about a mile. This is a loop that drops down into Solitude Creek and is several miles long. FS 122 rejoins FS 247 from the left in about another mile after you have crested over the first couple of hills and get a respite in a level and even downhill stretch. Continue on FS 247 to the base of Panorama Peak and a large steel gate. Some inexpensive power tools will take care of the gate (just kidding). Don't touch the gate. Just go around it with your bike through the fence on either side, as it is restricted to authorized motor travel and the fire tower at the top is off-limits. Just beyond the gate the grade becomes incredibly steep.

The climb to the top of Panorama Peak is as steep as anything outside of Moab, Utah, with merciful interruptions by water-diversion structures, or water bars, where one can stop and rest, then get started again. Grab a low gear and crank from water bar to water bar 'til you get to the top of the mountain at about the 3-mile point. At the top are meeting facilities that authorized guests can use for gatherings and an old Forest Service fire tower that is now privately owned. Stay clear of both of these, but take a breath, a picture, a drink, then head back.

After you go around the gate on the way back, there is a turnoff to the right on FS 247C that will drop you down toward Solitude Creek. This is a fun variation on the ride back, and there are a couple different routes that loop around and come back in on FS 122. A foot trail takes off to the east, traveling down all the way to Pinewood Lake as marked on the Forest Service map, but it goes through private land, and it is not known whether this land is accessible to bikes.

Explore all of the roads in this area and ride 'til you have had enough climbing, but be careful how far you drop into Solitude Creek, because it is a good climb out. This is a beautiful area and is not usually as crowded as the other rides in the region.

Pierson Park Road

Rating: Moderate to difficult

Distance: 15–20 miles round-trip

Time required: 2–4 hours

Notes: There are several variations that increase difficulty; a moderate ride without extra trails

Quadrangles: Longs Peak, Panorama Peak

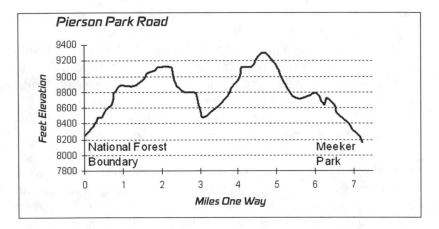

The Pierson Park Road parallels the Peak to Peak Highway (SH 7) to the east between Meeker Park and Estes Park. This is a four-wheel-drive road that connects up with several other roads that can also be cycled, but be aware of motor cycles and four-wheelers.

To reach Pierson Park Road, turn south on Fish Creek Road from US 36 just east of Estes Park at the east end of the causeway on the south side of Lake Estes. This lake is part of the Northwest Colorado Water Conservancy District and is fed by water diversion tunnels from the Colorado River drainage on the west side of the Continental Divide. Make note of the expense and environmental impact that comes with providing the Denver metro area its drinking water. Drive for about 3.5 miles on Fish Creek Road, then take a right onto Pierson Park Road and follow it through several switch-

Pierson Park Road

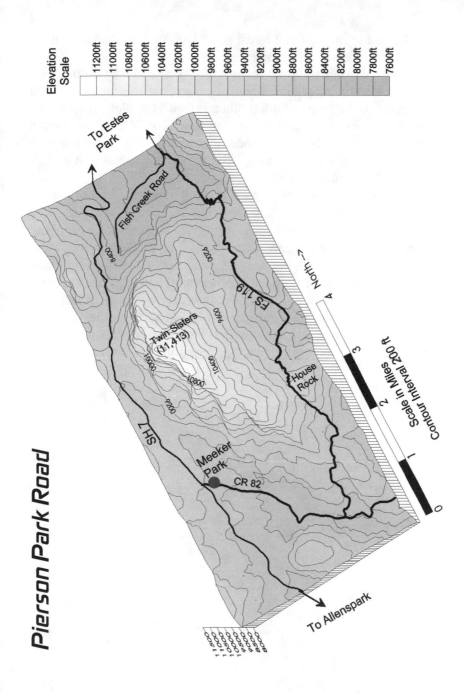

Elevation Scale

11200ft
11000ft
10800ft
10600ft
10400ft
10200ft
10000ft
9800ft
9600ft
9400ft
9200ft
9000ft
8800ft
8600ft
8400ft
8200ft
8000ft
7800ft
7600ft

To Estes Park

Fish Creek Road

8400

9200

FS 119

9400

9600

Twin Sisters (11,413)

10000

10600

10800

9200

North →

House Rock

Meeker Park

CR 82

SH 7

To Allenspark

Scale in Miles

0   1   2   3   4

Contour Interval 200 ft

11,500
11,000
10,500
10,000
9,500
9,000
8,500
8,000

backs and to the national forest boundary. Park in this area along the road and start riding south.

The Pierson Park Road is now FS 119 and climbs up the west side of Pierson Mountain. About 2 miles past the national forest boundary is the Pierson Park trailhead (Trail 949). Pierson Park Trail can be ridden all the way down Lion Gulch to Highway 36, though this is not normally recommended because it is very popular with hikers and equestrians. During fall afternoons this trail can be less crowded and thus more rideable.

Pierson Park Road rolls over small climbs and descents to the south past House Rock, a large rock outcrop on the east side of the road at about 5 miles, and finally drops into Meeker Park after about 8 miles. From here you can ride to the east on CR 82 to Johnny Park, another ride described in this book (see page 57), or turn right and take CR 82 west to SH 7, make another right, and head back to Estes Park. You can, of course, head back the way you came, especially if you parked at the national forest boundary. This ride is full of options and can be a good workout. It's also a good place to view the mountains and see wildlife like deer and elk.

Johnny Park

Rating: Difficult; hard and technical climb with smooth sections

Distance: 16 miles round-trip

Time required: 1–3 hours

Notes: Short distance but strenuous climb and many 4-wheel-drives and motorcycles

Quadrangles: Longs Peak, Panorama Peak

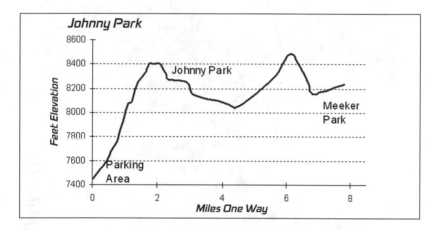

*T*he Johnny Park ride can be accessed either from US 36 between Lyons and Estes Park, or from the Peak to Peak Highway (SH 7) between Allenspark and Estes Park at Meeker Park. This is a hard though not horribly technical ride on a four-wheel-drive road that climbs steeply, then turns into more rolling terrain. It is fairly short, but a good workout. There can be a good deal of four-wheel-drive and motorcycle traffic on this road on summer weekends.

The route described here is from the east and is accessed from US 36. To reach the ride, drive to Lyons and take US 36 toward Estes Park (US 36 from Boulder to Estes Park is also a good road-bike ride). The highway follows the North St. Vrain Creek, which has cut a canyon through the Lyons Formation (reddish sandstone that is quarried and processed locally), for a couple miles, then departs

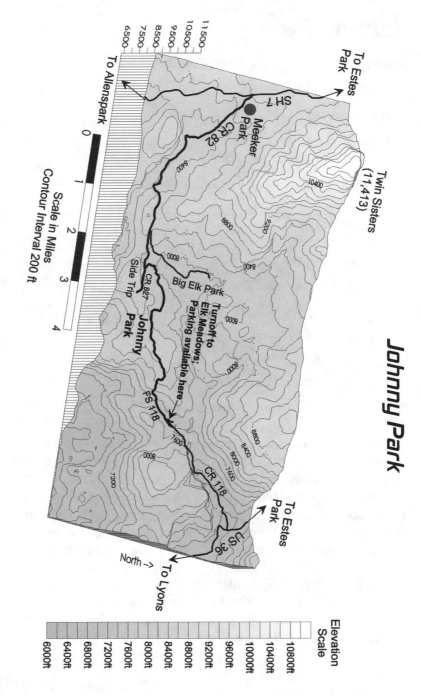

Johnny Park

Scale in Miles
Contour Interval 200 ft

Elevation Scale

and heads north to Little Elk Park. About 11 miles from Lyons the highway takes its first hard left turn, then, less than a mile later, a hard right. Just past the hard left, look for CR 118 on the left, which goes to Elk Meadows and Johnny Park. Drive up CR 118, a dirt road, for about 4 miles to the turnoff to the right to Elk Meadows. Park either at the fork in the road or farther up the hill at the next junction and begin riding to the southwest on CR 118.

The first mile of climbing is on the graveled and washboarded road, but at the top of the first hill CR 118 becomes FS 118, with lots of dirt and rocky four-wheel-drive road. For a side trip, turn left at the top of the hill and embark on a short but challenging climb up an old road; this is also good for one last climb before heading back to the car on the way back. Stay on the main road and climb on to the west. The climbing is mixed with flat stretches with water holes made ever wider by meandering four-wheel-drives. After about 4 miles you reach CR 82, on which you can head on into Meeker Park, or explore some of the trails that take off to the south (CR 827 and CR 828), or head back to the car the way you came. If you start the ride in Meeker Park, be careful how far you go because you will have to climb on the way back, though this is a fairly short ride and the return trip isn't terribly long. On this ride, always watch for hikers and horses, who have the right-of-way, and for motorcycles, which can come around corners at high speeds.

BOULDER
area

Boulder is located at the mouth of Boulder Canyon and can be the jumping-off point for several good rides as well as many more hiking trails. All of the rides around Boulder are associated with the nearby canyons, and some good workouts can include riding up the paved roads to a trailhead, riding the single track, then riding back down. This is sometimes necessary because of the short lengths of the single tracks.

Because of the University of Colorado and other factors, traffic can really be a problem in Boulder during times such as rush hour or during sporting events. Thus, it is a good idea to avoid peak hours on Saturdays and Sundays, and also avoid the downtown area if you are trying to get to a point across town. Foothills Parkway is the first exit off the Boulder Turnpike (US 36) coming north into Boulder from Denver, and this will take you around town and to Boulder Reservoir or back to Highway 36 via Jay Road. Highway 36 turns into 28th Street in Boulder, which can be very congested during rush hours.

The easiest way to get to Boulder Canyon and the rides that it leads to is to take US 36 north into town and take the Baseline Road exit. Turn west (left) on Baseline, then right on Broadway. You will crawl over "The Hill" and past the Boulder campus of the University of Colorado, but it isn't very far to Canyon Boulevard and signs directing you left to Nederland via Boulder Canyon. Broadway continues north and rejoins US 36 just north of town, from which you can reach Lefthand and St. Vrain Canyons, and the towns of Lyons and Estes Park. There is a plethora of bicycle shops in Boulder, but we have yet to receive enough free parts from any of them to recommend one.

Views of Boulder's scenic backdrop abound along the Reservoir's Open Space Trails.

There are several good trails that can be said to be in the Boulder area, though most are fairly technical and steep. We have searched for easier trails for the less-than-gonzo cyclist, but there aren't that many aside from the roads and trails around Boulder Reservoir. Note that there are plenty of rolling hills and trails that travel around the reservoir and through wetlands that provide a good workout with some good wildlife, and especially bird, viewing. The following trails are listed in order from north to south.

Rabbit Mountain Open Space Park

Rating: Moderate

Distance: 2–10 miles

Time required: 2 hours to all day

Notes: Gravel road with moderate side trails; new trails are also being constructed

Quadrangles: Carter Lake Reservoir, Hygiene

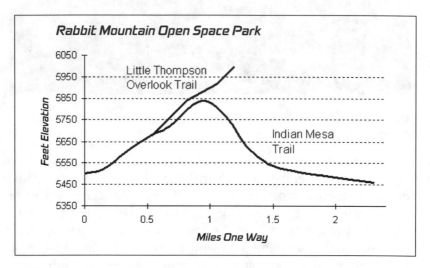

Rabbit Mountain Open Space Park

Feet Elevation vs *Miles One Way*

Little Thompson Overlook Trail

Indian Mesa Trail

Rabbit Mountain is rich in wildlife, plant life, geology, and history. The park is located in a transitional zone between the mountains and the plains. For this reason, the plants and animals are quite varied. Birds are plentiful in the park and include owls, hawks, falcons, eagles, various jays, flickers, and woodpeckers. Wildlife common to the park include mule and white-tailed deer, rattlesnakes, mountain lions (rarely seen, but tracks are visible on the trails), and many rodents such as voles, mice, and rabbits. Cactus, mountain mahogany, pine forest, and a wide range of grasses are also part of the Rabbit Mountain habitat.

The geology consists of sedimentary layers of sandstone, lime-

Rabbit Mountain Open Space Park

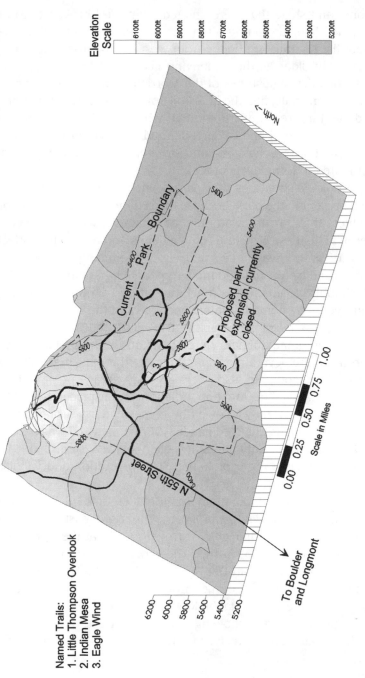

Named Trails:
1. Little Thompson Overlook
2. Indian Mesa
3. Eagle Wind

Elevation Scale

6100ft
6000ft
5900ft
5800ft
5700ft
5600ft
5500ft
5400ft
5300ft
5200ft

North

Current Park Boundary

Proposed park expansion, currently closed

N 55th Street

To Boulder and Longmont

Scale in Miles

0.00   0.25   0.50   0.75   1.00

stone, and shale that were uplifted, bent, and broken to form the hogback-like cuesta ridges that are so common in the Front Range foothills. As trails are ridden from west to east, rocks become progressively older as the underlying geological layers are exposed. This includes sandstones of the Morrison and Dakota Formations, the Benton shale, and the limestone of the Niobrara Formation. The sedimentary rocks were formed when sand (sandstone), mud (shale), and coral and calcareous mud (limestone) were deposited in ancient seas, coastal regions, or rivers and then compacted and cemented to form layers of rock.

Geologic structures such as synclines, hogbacks, and faults are also present in the park. Because the sedimentary layers act both as aquifers that transmit water and as aquitards, which are much less permeable, these structures create bends and breaks that affect the flow of groundwater, in some cases producing springs such as those used by ancient and modern people inhabiting the area.

Rabbit Mountain was inhabited off and on for over five thousand years by nomadic Native peoples, and the area was a winter hunting ground of the Arapaho tribe until the mid-1800s. Edible plants and game animals were abundant during prehistoric times, and there are several ancient springs in the park that still provide water. The mountain also offers a good vantage point to the surrounding lands. The Arapaho Indians were displaced by gold miners in the late 1850s, followed by homesteaders raising cattle and farming. The land changed hands several times and was finally sold to the Boulder County parks and open space system in 1984 after years of grazing and exploitation. The vegetation and wildlife are slowly making a comeback.

To reach Rabbit Mountain from Boulder, take US 36 north about 15 miles from Boulder toward Lyons. Turn right (east) at the railroad tracks onto SH 66 for 1 mile. Turn left (north) at the sign to Rabbit Mountain on North 55th Street. The park is located 2 miles along the road on the right. From Denver, take I-25 to the U.S. Highway 66/ Longmont exit. Follow US 66 through Longmont and drive another 12 miles to the sign to Rabbit Mountain on North 55th Street.

Start the ride by following North 53rd Street, off to the left side of the parking area, which runs along a large canal. The canal was built in 1959 as a diversion from Carter Lake, which in turn receives its water from the Western Slope lake of Granby through a series of tunnels under Rocky Mountain National Park.

Climb the hill, and at 0.5-mile there is a junction with several other trails. To the left is the .75-mile Little Thompson Overlook Trail. This trail climbs to the top of the northernmost ridge on a moderate trail over rocky soil and smooth sandstone bedrock. The road straight ahead continues for another 0.5-mile before it is restricted by private land.

Two other trails cut right from this intersection. The first is a trail that was under construction at the time of this writing. It is a moderate trail that traverses the hillside to the south and then cuts over the top of the ridge. The second is the 1.75-mile Indian Mesa Trail. The Indian Mesa Trail is actually a gravel road that heads south and gently climbs for 0.5-mile and then drops as it slowly turns north and terminates at private grazing land. Eagle Wind Trail intersects the Indian Mesa Trail at the 0.5-mile summit. Eagle Wind Trail climbs to the top of the ridge and continues for 1.5 miles (at the time of this writing) from the Indian Mesa Trail. The Eagle Wind Trail should be extended extensively due to the recent acquisition of new open space land on the southeast side of the park. The Eagle Wind Trail consists of loose rock and smooth sand/dirt.

Rabbit Mountain Park is a recent addition to the parks around the Denver metro area. It is small but contains several good trails fairly close to towns like Longmont, Boulder, Lyons, and Loveland. The attraction of this park is by no means limited to cycling. The trails are also fun to hike or run, and the sunrises and sunsets can be breathtaking. This is also a good place to watch the thunderstorms march off across northeastern Colorado, building in strength and ferocity as they go.

James Creek

Rating: Moderate; difficult if James Creek is ridden up and back; entire loop is very difficult

Distance: 6.5–9.5 miles

Time required: 2–4 hours

Notes: Very rocky; short but strenuous climbs and technical descents

Quadrangles: Gold Hill

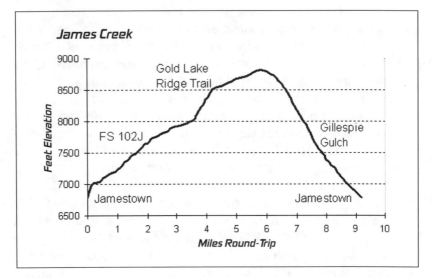

This ride crosses the ridge that serves as the drainage divide between the St. Vrain and Left Hand Canyons. It is on four-wheel-drive roads that skirt the west side of Walker Mountain. Left Hand Canyon and Creek are named for the Arapaho chief known as Chief Lefthand. His Arapaho name was actually *Niwot*, which is a local name for a town between Boulder and Longmont, a reservoir, and a peak on the Continental Divide. This ride threads in and out of private property, so stay on the trail and don't disturb any of the buildings or equipment you see along the way.

James Creek

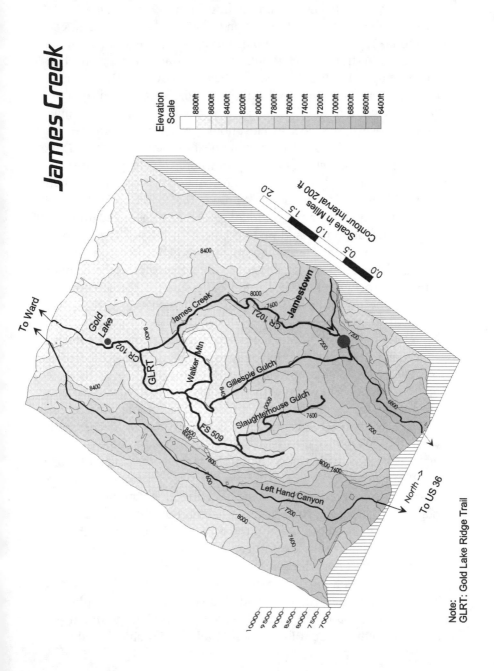

Elevation Scale

8800ft
8600ft
8400ft
8200ft
8000ft
7800ft
7600ft
7400ft
7200ft
7000ft
6800ft
6600ft
6400ft

Scale in Miles
0.0   0.5   1.0   1.5   2.0
Contour Interval 200 ft

To Ward

Gold Lake

CR 102

GLRT

James Creek

Walker Mtn

8400

8000

7600

CR 102J

Jamestown

7000

Gillespie Gulch

Slaughterhouse Gulch

7600

7200

FS 509

8400
8000

7600

Left Hand Canyon

8000

7600

7200

7600

North →
To US 36

6800

10000
9500
9000
8500
8000
7500
7000

Note:
GLRT: Gold Lake Ridge Trail

James Creek ○ 67

To reach the James Creek ride, travel north from Boulder on US 36 for about 5 miles, then turn left on Left Hand Canyon Road (CR 94) at Altona. This is also a good place to park and begin riding if you want a more strenuous workout. Left Hand Canyon is a great road-bike ride up to the Peak to Peak Highway. Follow Left Hand Canyon Road up Left Hand Canyon for about 6 miles to a fork in the road. Take the right (north) fork, James Canyon Road, for another 3 miles to Jamestown (7,100 feet in elevation). Park across from the post office on the south side of Main Street next to a small city park. There is a cafe across the street to the north where you can get water.

Ride west through town, past the post office, through a dip, over a speed bump, and turn left on Ward Road (CR 102J). This turn will designate the beginning of mileage measurement. Ward Road passes several houses and private land as it follows James Creek, staying on the west side. After a mile the road becomes washed out in many places, due to James Creek leaving its banks, and is therefore quite rocky and loose. During early summer the stream may actually flow down the road in this area, in which case a *portage* will be necessary.

At 1.8 miles there is an abandoned aqueduct, and at 2.4 miles a spur road to the right. Bear left, staying on Ward Road as it becomes somewhat more smooth and doesn't climb much over the next mile. At 3 miles you will ride past an old mine with rusted machinery and a large green shed. At 3.4 miles CR 102J fords James Creek, crossing to the east side. At the crossing it may be necessary to wade through part of the creek, though a log spans some of it. The water is shallow with a smooth bottom, making crossing fairly easy.

Ward Road continues to follow the river for a short distance before it turns south to climb a steep ravine to the top of Gold Lake ridge. Just before the road begins to climb out of the James Creek valley, you pass an old road on the right that is blocked with large boulders and a gate to keep trucks out. This old road is shown on some maps, but don't be confused—it is closed.

At 3.6 miles a small unnamed road takes off and climbs up a steep ravine to the left. This road climbs for 0.7-mile over difficult terrain to the top of the ridge just south of Walker Mountain and connects with the Gold Lake Ridge Trail, an old abandoned road,

2.1 miles after leaving CR 102J. This is an optional technical climb to the Gold Lake Ridge Trail.

Stay right on CR 102J. The road is rocky and steepens as it climbs out of the James Creek valley and into pine and aspen forest.

Gold Lake Ridge Trail is reached at 4.4 miles (8,500 feet in elevation). At this point the road is quite smooth as it gently descends to the east. As a side trip, turn right and ride for 4 miles (Gold Lake is 1 mile) to Ward (9,200 feet in elevation). Turn left on Gold Lake Ridge Trail and descend quickly down the smooth road for 1.3 miles to an intersection with the unnamed road at 2.1 miles north described previously that links to CR 102J. Turn right and take this route for the short but rough way back to Jamestown.

The easiest way back to Jamestown is to ride back the way you came on Gold Lake Ridge Trail to CR 102J. For a technical descent, ride a short distance forward on Gold Lake Ridge Trail to a fork. Take the left fork and ride west to where two switchbacks and a steep 3.5-mile single-track descent takes you down Gillespie Gulch to Jamestown. Once at Jamestown continue straight ahead to Main Street. Take a left and ride through town and back to your car at 9.2 total miles.

For additional rides in the area, or if you miss the turn down Gillespie Gulch, Gold Lake Ridge Trail continues to descend gradually for another 0.7-mile and then descends steeply down loose rock for 1.3 more miles before coming to a large hill. Along this ridge there are good views of Left Hand Canyon, the town of Rowena, Bighorn Mountain and its many mines to the south, and Boulder to the east. The trail splits in three directions here. To the left (north) is a technical descent down Slaughterhouse Gulch back to Jamestown. There's a private property sign halfway down Slaughterhouse Gulch, so this trail is not recommended. The trail in the middle is an unrideable climb straight up to the top of Nugget Hill. This vantage point offers good views of Boulder and the plains before the trail ends. To the right is a very steep and very technical descent down to the town of Rowena, at 9.1 miles. From Rowena you would have to ride east on Left Hand Canyon Road to the James Canyon Drive junction, turn left, and ride back up to Jamestown for 7 miles on the highway and a total 16.1 miles.

Boulder Reservoir
Open Space Rides

Rating: Easy, with one moderate to difficult climb

Distance: Variable

Time required: 1 hour or more

Notes: Nontechnical with rolling topography

Quadrangles: Boulder, Niwot

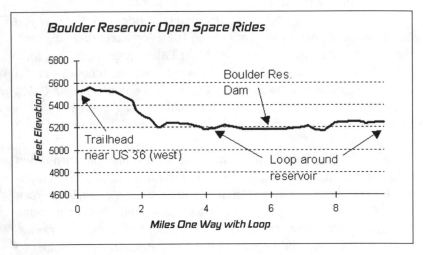

Boulder Reservoir Open Space Rides

Boulder Reservoir is located northeast of Boulder and provides miles of easy and moderate trails through wetlands and rolling topography. Birds of prey and migratory waterfowl can be seen during different times of the year. This open space park is also open to riding, running, and hiking for most of the year, with snow covering the trails from December to April or May. Wind can be a deterrent to riding in the colder months.

There are two convenient ways to get to the trails around Boulder Reservoir. To park on the reservoir's east side, drive north through Boulder on Foothills Parkway to where it turns into SH 119, or the Diagonal Highway, to Longmont. Just northeast of Boulder

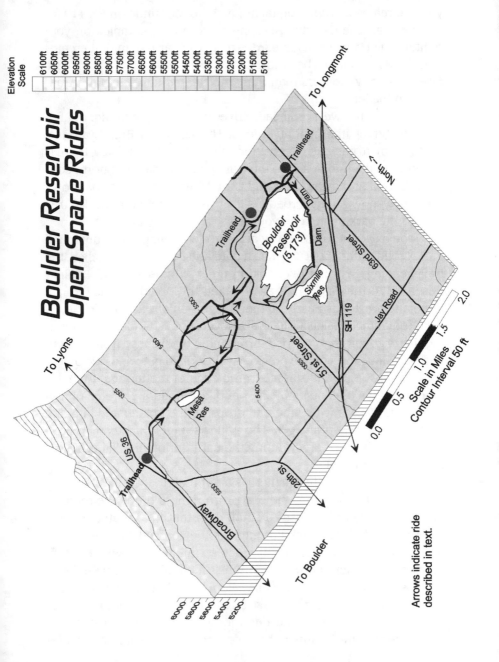

Elevation Scale

6100ft 6050ft 6000ft 5950ft 5900ft 5850ft 5800ft 5750ft 5700ft 5650ft 5600ft 5550ft 5500ft 5450ft 5400ft 5350ft 5300ft 5250ft 5200ft 5150ft 5100ft

Boulder Reservoir
Open Space Rides

To Longmont

To Lyons

To Boulder

Trailhead

Trailhead

Trailhead

Trailhead

Boulder Reservoir (5,173)

Sixmile Res.

Dam

Dam

Mesa Res.

North →

63rd Street

SH 119

Jay Road

51st Street

28th St.

US 36

Broadway

5300

5400

5500

5400

5300

5500

5500

6000
5800
5600
5400
5200

Scale in Miles

0.0   0.5   1.0   1.5   2.0

Contour Interval 50 ft

Arrows indicate ride
described in text.

you will reach the traffic signal at Jay Road. Continue on SH 119 for 2 miles, past the Celestial Seasonings corporate complex on your right, to the traffic signal at 63rd Street. The earth dam that creates Boulder Reservoir will be visible on the left (north). Turn left on 63rd Street and drive for less than a mile to the parking area for a trail-head on the left (west).

To reach the west trailhead, drive north through Boulder either on 28th Street (the continuation of US 36) or on Broadway. Just north of town, past the intersection of US 36 and Broadway, there is a turnoff to the right (east) to the trailhead that is on the north con-tinuation of Broadway. Turn right and follow the continuation of Broadway, now a gravel road, as it turns back to the north for 0.3-mile to the parking area on your left.

Ride back out to Broadway and turn left, riding on an unnamed gravel road. After about .25-mile a gate and trailhead is reached, the trail heading east and overlooking creeks, marshes, and Boulder Reservoir to the east. The trail is called the Boulder Valley Ranch Trail, and it extends nearly all the way to Boulder Reservoir.

From either trailhead there are several trails to explore, includ-ing the reservoir itself. To ride through the open space from west to east, continue through the previously described gate and ride on the trail across the upland surface to the edge of the terrace. After 1.6 miles from the parking lot the first and last moderate stretch of trail is reached. This is where the trail drops off the upland and into one of the intermittent drainages. The trail is straight but steep and can be muddy if it's wet, or icy during the early spring or fall, because it is shaded by the hill.

At the bottom of the hill there is a dirt road that the Boulder Val-ley Ranch Trail follows to the east. Turn right and ride the road for 0.8-mile to where it crosses a small dam that has created a small reservoir and climbs back up onto another upland surface. At the top of this moderate climb you reach a trail junction where a trail takes off to the left (north). Continue straight ahead for 0.5-mile to the east end of the Boulder Valley Ranch Trail at 2.9 miles. This is the Eagle trailhead at north 51st Street, a gravel north-south road. Turn left on 51st Street and ride along the road as it crosses the upland for 0.5-mile, turns right, dropping into the small valley created by Dry Creek, then turns north again for 0.5-mile and begins to climb to the north. Just as 51st Street starts to turn north, the Boulder Valley Ranch Trail begins again at a trailhead just off the right (east) side of the road. Take this trail and ride along the north side of Boulder Reservoir for 1 mile toward the easternmost trailhead. Along this stretch of trail you will cross an inlet canal for Boulder Reservoir. This is a dangerous structure because it is a bridge over a concrete canal just north of where it drops through a flow-controlling cascade of concrete blocks. The bridge is, however, equipped with railing and a fence, so if you heed the signs that inform you of impending doom upon entering the canal, you will be just fine.

About .25-mile before you reach the easternmost trailhead, after you cross the inlet canal for the Boulder Reservoir, there is an unnamed trail that takes off to the right and heads for the dam. Ride on this trail to the south and cross the dam after about 0.5-mile. At the south end of the dam you will ride through the marina area to the recreation area entrance and back to the west to 51st Street again at 5.5 miles.

Turn right (north) on 51st Street and follow the gravel road for 0.7-mile, dropping and crossing Dry Creek once again and reaching the trailhead for the Boulder Valley Ranch Trail on the left (west), which you have seen before. Turn into the parking area, ride onto the trail, and head back to the west on Boulder Valley Ranch Trail. Ride back the way you came, up a moderate climb. On the way back this stretch of trail may seem more like a difficult climb, and there's no reason to feel bad if you have to walk it. After you have made it up the last climb, the trail is a gradual climb back to the parking lot and trailhead for a total of 9.2 miles.

Sourdough Trail

Rating: Moderate to difficult

Distance: 7.5 miles one way or 16-mile loop

Time required: 2 hours one way or 4 hours for loop

Notes: Very rocky trail; good climbs through forest at 10,000 feet

Quadrangles: Ward

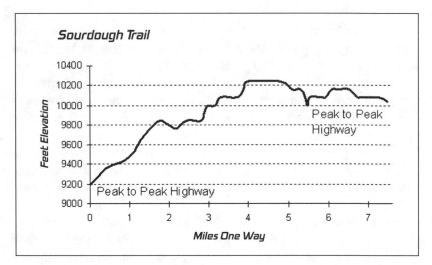

*T*he Sourdough Trail (FS Trail 835) is a Boulder classic, most likely one of the first trails people ride after they move into their over-priced Boulder condominiums. The loop described here is a ride on the Sourdough Trail with a return trip on the Peak to Peak Highway.

To reach the trailhead, take Canyon Boulevard west from Boulder and up Boulder Canyon (SH 119) to Nederland. Head north at the roundabout onto the Peak to Peak Highway (SH 72) toward Ward. Drive north on SH 72 for about 9 miles to CR 116 (at the University of Colorado Mountain Research Station). Turn left onto CR 116 and drive for 0.5-mile to the Sourdough trailhead. You can park here and begin riding.

Sourdough Trail

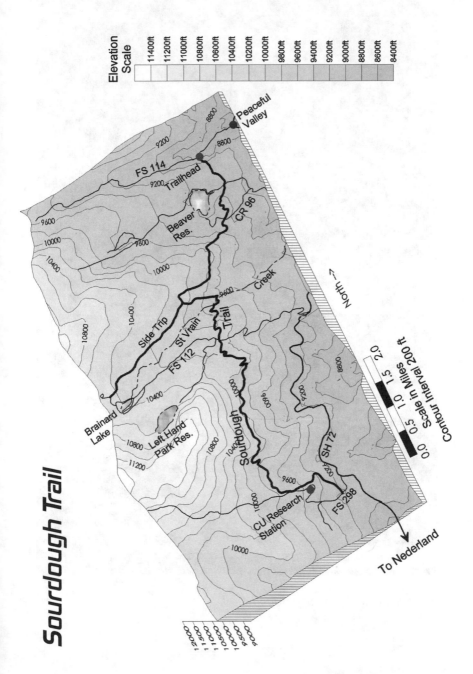

A waterfall along the Sourdough Trail.

From the trailhead the trail climbs up through the forest for the first 3 miles with several switchbacks. The trail is rocky at best for most of this distance. Some smooth sections exist for the next 4 miles as the trail levels somewhat and begins a downhill before one final climb to the Brainard Lake Road. The trail intersects the Brainard Lake Road 3 miles west of the Peak to Peak Highway and just before the fee station to Brainard Lake and the Indian Peaks. A side trip here will take you up to Brainard Lake on a paved road, though there is a fee to enter the area.

The trail can now be ridden back the way you came, or you can take a right on Brainard Lake Road and descend through hairpin curves to the Peak to Peak Highway. Brainard Lake Road is steep with several tight corners for a fast and exhilarating coast. Once at the Peak to Peak Highway, take a right (south) and ride the remaining 7 miles.

Another option from Brainard Lake Road is to cross the road and continue on the Sourdough Trail, dropping into the St. Vrain drainage. You will reach St. Vrain Creek in about a mile on a single track that is *very* steep, with *very* large boulders. After crossing the creek, the trail climbs on to the northwest and joins the Wapiti Trail (FS Trail 816) in about .75-mile. Take a right on the trail and ride north for only about .25-mile to another junction, this time with the Baptist Trail (FS Trail 815). Take a right and ride for about a mile, descending to the trailhead at CR 96. From here you can descend on the improved road to the Peak to Peak Highway, again turning right (south), and take the highway back to where you began. This time, though, the distance on the highway is closer to 10 miles.

The Peak to Peak Highway is not a great disappointment to ride after riding the single-track trails. There are lots of great views, a decent shoulder, and places to stop and get food. It is at a fairly high elevation, averaging around 9,000 feet, and climbs and drops enough to remind you of this. Thus, the highway is also a good workout in mountain surroundings.

Switzerland Trail

Rating: Easy to moderate

Distance: 26 miles round-trip

Time required: 3–4 hours

Notes: Old railroad grade allows for easy inclines but climbs are long; nothing really technical

Quadrangles: Gold Hill

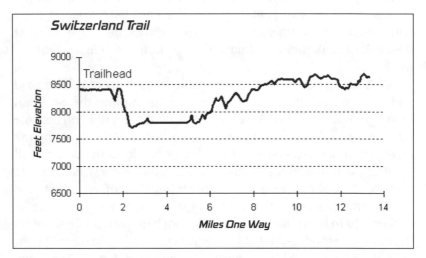

Switzerland Trail

*T*he grade of an old railroad, the Switzerland Trail, now FS 327, is a popular out-and-back trip from Sugarloaf Road to Sawmill Road, or it can be a shorter loop that involves a technical descent into Pennsylvania Gulch and then a climb back up. Either route provides good views and a decent workout. This ride is called a trail, though it is actually a road.

To reach the trail, drive west up Boulder Canyon (SH 119) for about 7 miles to Sugarloaf Road (CR 122). Take a right (north) and follow Sugarloaf Road for about 10 miles to where Sugarloaf Mountain Road takes off to the right. Follow Sugarloaf Mountain Road for about 2 miles to the well-marked trailhead. There is normally ample parking at the trailhead, but please try not to park off the designated

Switzerland Trail

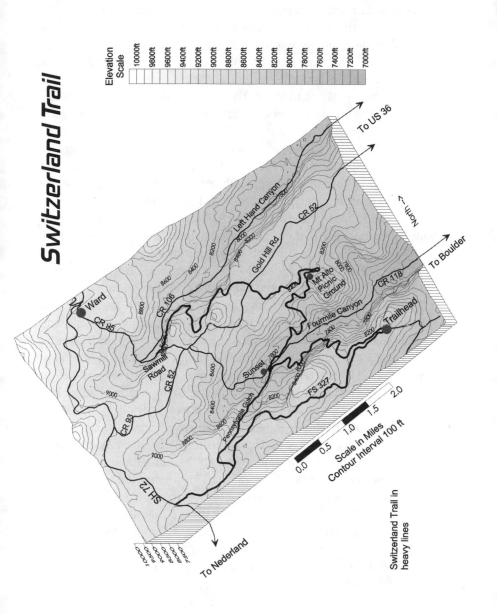

Elevation Scale

10000ft
9800ft
9600ft
9400ft
9200ft
9000ft
8800ft
8600ft
8400ft
8200ft
8000ft
7800ft
7600ft
7400ft
7200ft
7000ft

To US 36

To Boulder

North

Left Hand Canyon

CR 52

Gold Hill Rd

Mt Alto Picnic Ground

CR 118

Fourmile Canyon

Trailhead

Ward

CR 95

CR 106

CR 52

Sawmill Road

CR 93

Sunset

Pennsylvania Gulch

FS 327

SH 72

To Nederland

Scale in Miles
0.0 0.5 1.0 1.5 2.0
Contour Interval 100 ft

Switzerland Trail in heavy lines

areas and damage the vegetation. The fire danger in this area, as with most of the lower elevations of the Front Range, is high for most of the year, so be careful with fire of any kind. Be aware, as well, of a less than obvious fire hazard, the catalytic converter of your car when it is parked over tall dry grass.

The narrow gauge railroad, the remnants of which you will be riding on, was a connection between Boulder and mining camps in the mountains for shipping and holiday getaways. It originally began at the intersection of Broadway and Canyon Boulevard in Boulder. It was constructed in 1883 and named the Denver, Salt Lake & Pacific Railroad, though its maximum length was only about 35 miles, reaching only the small towns of Ward, Cardinal, and Eldora. The railroad survived until 1919 but was finally closed, predominantly because of damaging floods, including the great flood of 1894, which also swept through downtown Boulder.

Leaving the trailhead, ride down a short road on the north side of the ridge where you parked. This leads to the Switzerland Trail (FS 327). The old grade is rocky and rough, though fairly flat and nontechnical. There can be pretty good sized puddles, though, and thunderstorms can sneak up on you here. This trail winds around for about 13 miles before reaching Sawmill Road. The final climb to Sawmill Road is very technical and you may well turn around before you reach it. The road meets up with the Switzerland Trail in less than a mile. You can turn right to ride the whole trail or turn left to take a short trip to the Peak to Peak Highway.

To take the shorter side trip up to the Peak to Peak Highway, bear left at the junction and ride west on the fairly flat grade. This is actually the continuation of the railroad grade that the trail follows. After about 4 miles you'll come to a turnoff to the right for Pennsylvania Gulch. Turn right, and be ready for a challenge, because the trail drops very steeply here. After about 4.5 miles the trail cuts through private land, so don't leave the trail or even look at any of the private trees because they don't belong to you. The Peak to Peak Highway is about a mile from the Pennsylvania Gulch turnoff, a ride of a little less than 5.5 miles. The return trip is for the most part a gradual downhill.

The longer ride to the north on the Switzerland Trail is an out-and-back ride that rolls and winds through the pine forest to the east and is lower in elevation than the Peak to Peak Highway. At the initial junction mentioned above, take a right onto the Switzerland Trail as it turns back west and drops gradually for about 3 miles to Four Mile Creek. Here, the Switzerland Trail turns back to the east and climbs past the enclave of Sunset, a junction with CR 118, and heads for the Mount Alto Picnic Area, another 2.5 miles ahead. Ride on past the picnic area and through another hairpin turn as the Switzerland Trail heads west and north for 1.5 miles to CR 52, or Gold Hill Road. This road connects the town of Gold Hill to the east with the Peak to Peak Highway to the west. Past Gold Hill Road the trail drops some as it skirts the southern rim of Left Hand Canyon. Ride for about 1.5 miles to Sawmill Road and turn around. Ride back the way you came—there are no other worthy options for returning to your vehicle.

Betasso Preserve

Rating: Easy to moderate

Distance: 3 miles

Time required: 20 minutes to 1 hour

Notes: Short ride with quick descents through forest and open meadows with sweeping views of Boulder and plains

Quadrangles: Boulder

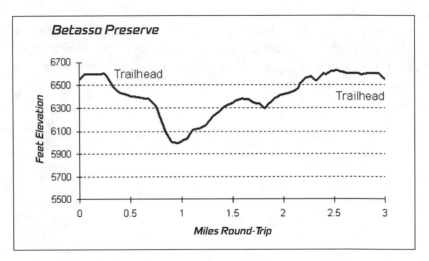

*T*he Betasso Preserve is one of many ranches along the Front Range that have been set aside as open space parks, offering forest and open-meadow environments with sweeping views of the Indian Peaks to the west and Boulder and the plains to the east. The picnic facilities are very nice, with covered tables, grills, and a pit toilet. Groups of up to fifty people can reserve the site for picnics. For further information, group picnics, or requests for interpretive programs, phone the Boulder County Parks and Open Space Department at 441-3950.

To reach the preserve, take Canyon Boulevard (SH 119) west out of Boulder, following Boulder Canyon for 7miles to Sugarloaf Road. Turn right on Sugarloaf Road and climb for less than a mile

Betasso Preserve

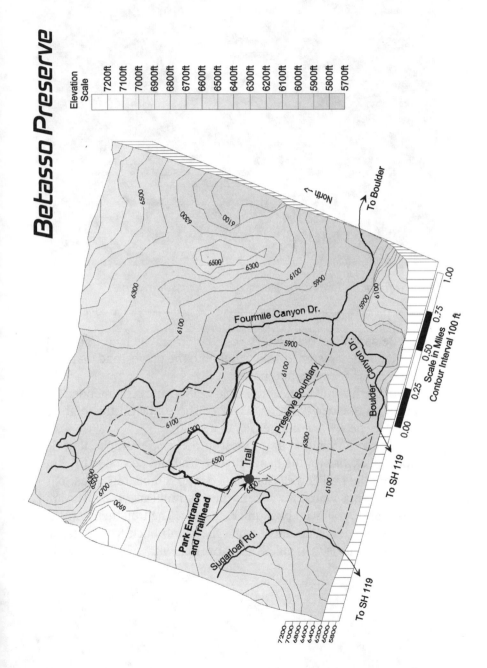

Elevation Scale

7200ft
7100ft
7000ft
6900ft
6800ft
6700ft
6600ft
6500ft
6400ft
6300ft
6200ft
6100ft
6000ft
5900ft
5800ft
5700ft

To Boulder

North ←

Fourmile Canyon Dr.

Preserve Boundary

Boulder Canyon Dr.

To SH 119

Trail

Park Entrance and Trailhead

Sugarloaf Rd.

To SH 119

Scale in Miles
Contour Interval 100 ft

0.00   0.25   0.50   0.75   1.00

A late-afternoon ride in the forest of the Betasso Preserve.

to the Betasso Preserve sign. Follow the directions by turning right and, after a short distance, take a left onto the gravel road that leads to the Betasso Preserve and park.

Though this trail is close to Boulder, it is not recommended that you ride up Boulder Canyon (SH 119). The traffic on this highway can be very heavy and dangerous to cyclists.

From the parking area, go west at the loop entrance and ride the loop clockwise for the best ride (the trail can be ridden in either direction). The trail is well maintained, and a moderately fast pace is possible—but watch for hikers on this multi-use trail. The trail climbs slightly, followed by a quick descent. The trail then contours around a steep hillside and begins the climb back to the starting point. The trail is 2.9 miles long overall with a total elevation change of 440 feet.

Walker Ranch Loop

Rating: Difficult because of climbs and technical stretches

Distance: 7-mile off-road loop, 16 from Boulder and back including loop

Time required: About 3–4 hours

Notes: This trail drops fast, then climbs straight back up; watch for hikers and other cyclists

Quadrangles: Eldora Springs

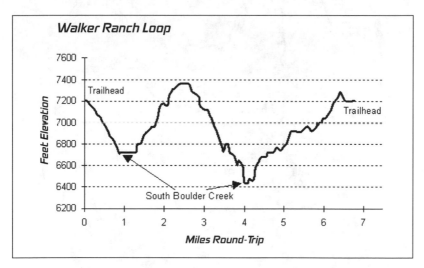

W alker Ranch Open Space Park is named for an old ranch homestead in the foothills west of Boulder. This ride is popular because it is challenging and within biking distance of Boulder.

To reach the park, take the Baseline Road exit off the Boulder Turnpike (US 36), turn left at the light, and follow Baseline west across Broadway. Stay on Baseline as it climbs past Chautauqua Park and out of town. At this point Baseline Road turns into Flagstaff Road and climbs the very steep grade of Flagstaff Hill. Watch out for cyclists on Flagstaff Road. For a serious workout, park at the bottom of the hill and ride all the way to the ranch and back.

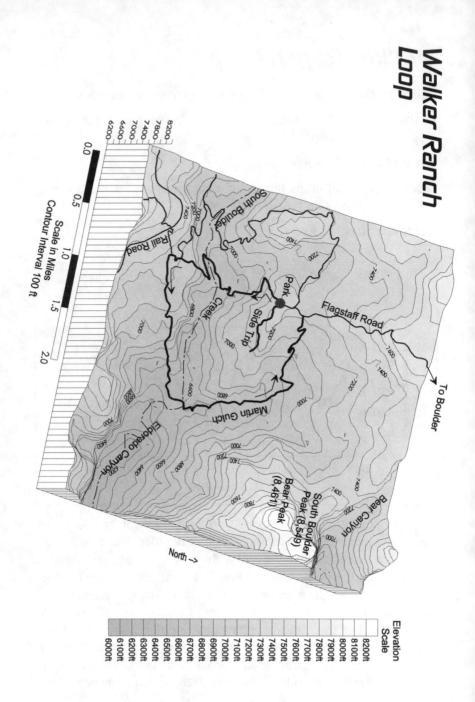

Turn left off Flagstaff Road and onto a dirt road marked by a sign indicating Walker Ranch. This turnoff is just before Flagstaff Road turns sharply to the west. The trailhead is about a quarter of a mile away. Park at the trailhead and ride south down the single track toward South Boulder Creek. The trail drops in elevation quickly as it switchbacks down the rocky slopes, though it's not especially technical. After about a mile you are at South Boulder Creek and crossing a wooden footbridge. The trail follows South Boulder Creek for 0.5-mile, then heads up the south side of the canyon. This is a grueling climb that pauses briefly at a hairpin turn at the 2-mile mark. The climb continues through technical and very steep sections for another mile to Gross Dam Road. Take a left, continuing on the trail, and ride over the ridge and down to the east. After about .25-mile there is a left turnoff to a picnic area at the top of a small knob. Continue to the east and straight ahead. The trail here is not very technical, but you will soon reach a few tricky switchbacks and a couple of technical descents. The trail continues to drop until you reach a point where it drops over the edge of the gorge at the 5-mile mark. Here you must carry your bike down over rocks and through slide rock to reach the creek, where you will again find a rideable trail and cross a bridge over South Boulder Creek, heading east toward the return trip up Martin Gulch.

The return trail is an old road and thus in places more of a road than a trail. It is a continuous climb—not very technical, but a strenuous climb nonetheless. Follow the trail to the top of the canyon, where, at about 6.25 miles, it joins an unmarked improved gravel road that heads left, winding through scattered houses and back to the Flagstaff Road. Take this road, and you will reach the paved Flagstaff Road about .25-mile north from the turnoff. From here you can either turn left and head back to the trailhead if your car is parked there, or turn right for Boulder if you chose the more challenging ride from the bottom of Flagstaff Hill.

Community Ditch Trail

Rating: Easy

Distance: 3–8 miles

Time required: 1–2 hours

Notes: Be careful at the SH 93 crossing

Quadrangles: Eldorado Springs, Superior

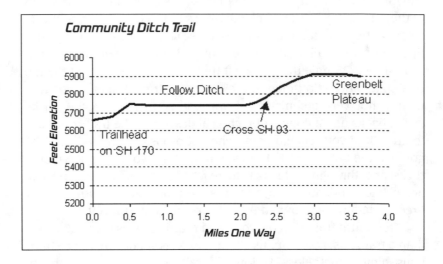

J ust south of Boulder is a small area with some easily accessible and easy (and we mean *easy*) rides. A good number of the trails in this area follow the Community Ditch, a water conveyance canal that once carried water from the South Boulder Creek drainage near Eldorado Springs to agricultural areas to the east.

To reach the Community Ditch Trail, drive south from the Boulder city limits on SH 93 toward Golden for 1.5 miles to a set of traffic lights at the intersection with SH 170. At this intersection, turn right (west) on SH 170, toward Eldorado Springs. At about 1.25 miles on SH 170 there is a parking area on the right for hikers only of Boulder Mountain Parks. Immediately after this on the left (south) side of the road is a well-marked open space trailhead to the lower end of the Community Ditch.

Community Ditch Trail

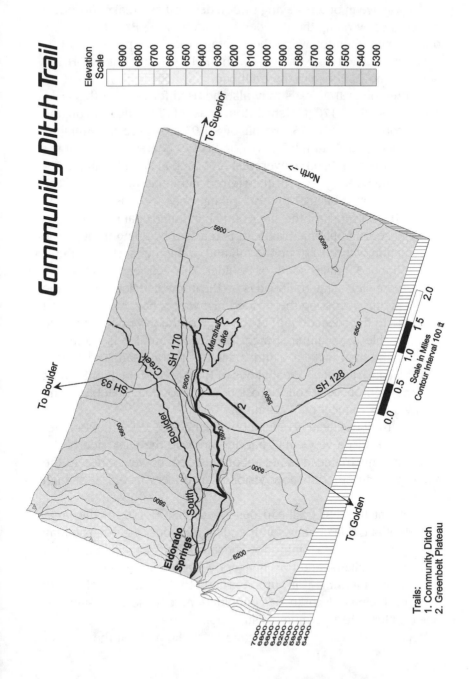

Elevation Scale

6900 6800 6700 6600 6500 6400 6300 6200 6100 6000 5900 5800 5700 5600 5500 5400 5300

To Superior

North ←

To Boulder

SH 93

SH 170

Boulder Creek

Marshall Lake

SH 128

South

Eldorado Springs

To Golden

5800

5800

5800

5800

5800

5800

6000

6200

5800

7000
6800
6600
6400
6200
6000
5800
5600
5400

0.0   0.5   1.0   1.5   2.0

Scale in Miles
Contour Interval 100 ft

Trails:
1. Community Ditch
2. Greenbelt Plateau

If you live in or are staying in Boulder, you can make this ride a bit tougher by riding the Boulder bike path along Broadway south out of town, then following the frontage road that parallels SH 93 for about a mile to the junction with SH 170. Turn right on SH 170 and ride the 1.25-mile to the trailhead.

Three other trailheads may also be used for rides in this area. The first is off SH 170 (Marshall Road) east of Eldorado Canyon and the second is on SH 128 just off of SH 93. To reach the Marshall Road parking area, turn left (east) on SH 170 (Marshall Road) at the intersection with SH 93. Travel west on Marshall Road for about .75-mile to the parking area on the right (south) side of the road. The trail is split into biking-only and hiking-only sections as the trail climbs the hillside past the site of an abandoned coal mine.

The second optional trailhead is reached by going through the intersection with SH 170 up the hill and to the intersection with SH 128 at about 3.3 miles south of Boulder. Turn left (east) on SH 128. The Greenbelt Plateau trailhead is on the immediate left. At the time of this writing, crossing the divided highway is hazardous in small cars due to the steep dropoff at the edge of the pavement. It would be advisable to continue straight on SH 128 until it is no longer divided and then make a U-turn back to the trailhead. The Green-belt Plateau Trail offers great views of Boulder and the Front Range and the Flatirons as it rolls across the fields on Marshall Mesa and finally drops to meet the Community Ditch Trail.

The third trailhead is reached by taking SH 93 south of Boulder for 1.8 miles to a very small parking area on the west side of the highway. This trailhead is not recommended, however, due to the small parking area and low visibility of drivers traveling at high speeds.

Park at the first trailhead described, on SH 170, at the large gravel lot and ride directly south and up a gradual incline. You may have other trail users joining you, because this area is popular with equestrians, hikers, and trail runners. After about .25-mile there is a picnic area and the trail turns abruptly to the east. Dowdy Draw Trail, for hiking only, branches due south here. Follow the sign and ride on along the Community Ditch Trail.

As you ride along, you can gaze off to the north at the Boulder

Boulder's Flatirons show their southern profiles to riders on the Community Ditch Trail.

valley and the Flatirons. These rocks were formed when rivers eroded the ancestral Rocky Mountains and deposited the resulting sand and gravel in broad, extensive alluvial fans and river channels that were fairly flat. The sediment became cemented into what we now call the Fountain Formation, and when the Front Range was uplifted, the rocks were bent and broken as they were tilted to the orientation you now see. Erosion has continued to work on the mountains, removing the rock that was once on top of the Front Range and leaving the exposed tilted beds that we call the Flatirons. It is now time to redirect your gaze at the trail before you tumble into the ditch.

This ride is cut into two sections by SH 93 at the point where it crosses the ditch. The crossing is 2 miles from the trailhead, and, depending on your party and the time of day, you may want to turn back here. The trail crosses SH 93 near a corner, and there are three lanes of absolutely insane commuters driving at absurd speeds and passing one another with little apparent regard for safety. This notwithstanding, it is possible to wait until there is a break in the traffic and cross the road. Just remember that the cars are coming fast, so you need a large head start.

On the east side of SH 93 is the Marshall Mesa Open Space Park. The trail now splits, with the Greenbelt Plateau Trail starting about 15 yards south of the Community Ditch Trail on the east side of SH 93. You can continue on either trail.

The Greenbelt Plateau Trail climbs about 200 feet over a smooth sand road to the top of Marshall Mesa. The mesa top offers great views of the Boulder Flatirons and Boulder. At 0.3-mile a short, moderately difficult trail to the left (north) descends the Mesa to connect back with the Community Ditch Trail after 0.2-mile. The Greenbelt Plateau Trail continues for another 1.3 miles with little elevation change through rolling grass prairie to the trailhead on SH 128.

The Community Ditch Trail from the east side of SH 93 contours Marshall Mesa and offers good views of Boulder and the Flatirons. At 0.4-mile an intersection with a steep, moderately difficult trail to the right heads to the Greenbelt Plateau Trail after 0.2-mile. After another 0.1-mile, a hiking-only trail spurs to the left and ultimately meets the Community Ditch Trail at Marshall Road. The Community Ditch Trail continues to the right for another mile before it drops quickly over some rocky sections to the Marshall Road parking area after 1.3 miles. Just before the trail descends there is a short walk to Marshall Lake, which is actually a reservoir, where the Community Ditch empties into it.

As you ride on the Community Ditch Trail, look at the foreground to the north, toward SH 170 and the road that becomes Cherryvale Road climbing up the opposite ridge. The ridge is bare of vegetation in places and sandstone can be seen there. Look at the road taking off to the north and notice that on the east side of it there are a number of depressions that are in almost a checkerboard pattern. This area has been affected by the coal mining of the early part of the twentieth century that was responsible for the existence of the towns of Marshall, Superior, Lafayette, and others in the area. Miners removed coal from sedimentary beds below the sandstone, taking as much as possible while leaving pillars of coal to support the mine roofs.

As a mine was abandoned the pillars were sometimes removed, and the *adits,* or mine entrances, were blocked. Years later, the sandstone and other rocks caved in or sagged into the mine workings. What you see to the north are areas where coal was removed and the mines collapsed. There are many areas in Boulder County where mine subsidence has been measured, though this is the only place where the phenomenon is this pronounced at the surface. In most other areas the coal was deeper and covered by more flexible shale layers, and the mining caused only subtle depressions in the ground surface. The amount of damage at the surface is proportional to the depth of the mine and the thickness of the layers of coal removed.

Eldorado Canyon State Park and the town of Eldorado Springs to the west can be seen from nearly all the trails described here. Eldorado Springs and Canyon have been a tourist destination for many years. Dwight D. Eisenhower and his wife, Mamie, honeymooned here at the beginning of World War I. The springs water is bottled and sold in the area and is also used to fill a refreshingly chilly pool at the resort. The canyon is renowned for its rock climbing—it's referred to as "Eldo" by the locals. There is also a short, steep, and somewhat technical mountain bike ride in Eldorado Canyon called Rattlesnake Gulch. The trail is very short and requires a Boulder Parks pass, $1 per bike per day to get in. For these reasons it has not been included here.

Rollins Pass

Rating: Difficult to very difficult

Distance: 30 miles to pass and back; 65 miles to Winter Park and
back

Time required: 3–8 hours

Notes: This ride is long and the trail/road is rough, with lots of
elevation change between 9,000 and 12,000 feet

Quadrangles: Fraser, East Portal, Nederland

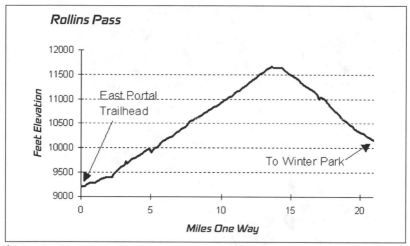

(Note: elevation profile does not show entire ride.)

Rollins Pass is the remnants of an old railroad grade that once
connected Denver on the east to Winter Park on the west. The
historic Moffat Tunnel now provides a subterranean shortcut for the
railroad, but the view is much better from the road. This ride is a
good place to try out bike camping or to ride over into Winter Park
to stay the night, returning the next day. There are also plenty of
rides in the Winter Park area if you want to spend some time over
there before returning, but remember that the climb back to the eastern side of the mountain is not trivial. For an easier and picturesque
ride, you might want to ride just to the summit of the pass and

Rollins Pass

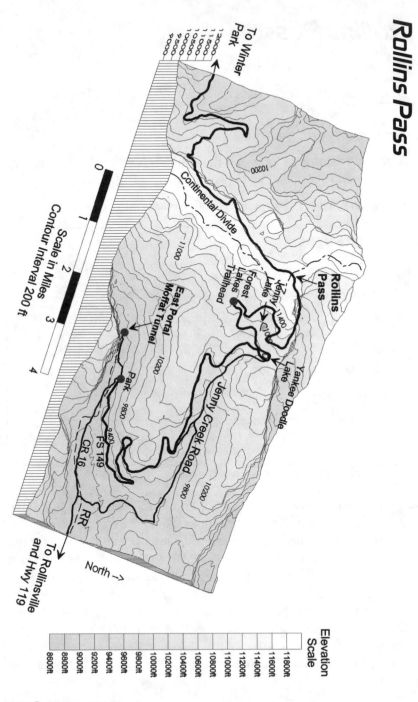

To Winter
Park

Continental Divide

Rollins
Pass

Jenny
Lake

Forest
Lakes
Trailhead

11000

11400

Yankee Doodle
Lake

Jenny Creek Road

East Portal
Moffat Tunnel

10200

Park

9800

9400

9800

10200

CR 16

FS 149

RR

To Rollinsville
and Hwy 119

North →

0   1   2   3   4

Scale in Miles
Contour Interval 200 ft

Elevation
Scale

11800ft
11600ft
11400ft
11200ft
11000ft
10800ft
10600ft
10400ft
10200ft
10000ft
9800ft
9600ft
9400ft
9200ft
9000ft
8800ft
8600ft

96 ○ Boulder Area

observe the changing aspen in the fall, then ride back. The railroad is still active, with trains using the Moffat Tunnel between Rollinsville and Winter Park, so be careful and watch for railroad employees in that area.

Rollinsville was founded in the early 1870s as a gateway to the Rollinsville and Middle Park Toll Road developed by John Quincy Adams Rollins, who constructed the first quartz mill to concentrate gold ore from local mines. He found that the real gold was in failed claims and began purchasing them. By 1880 Rollins had accumulated nearly 20,000 linear feet of gold-bearing veins, three hundred placer claims, and 2,000 acres of farmland. Around the turn of the century, David Moffat obtained the right-of-way and built the railway over Rollins Pass that is, for the most part, used for this ride. This was of course temporary, because in 1928 he built the tunnel that bears his name. The Rollins Pass route climbed over the top of the Front Range, using thirty-three tunnels and two huge trestles. The only tunnel on this route that is still in existence is the Needle Eye Tunnel, near the summit, and it is closed because of cave-ins. This tunnel is in an unusual location, perched above a huge drop-off overlooking the Great Plains from above timberline, and it cuts through a thin ridge. There are no remaining trestles.

To reach Rollins Pass from the east, drive from Boulder to Nederland via Boulder Canyon on SH 119, and then head south on the Peak to Peak Highway (SH 119) for about 5 miles to the turnoff for Rollinsville on CR 16. Turn right (west) on CR 16 and drive through Rollinsville. Continue on up this dusty, bumpy road for about 5 more miles to the turnoff on the right to FS 149. Park either at this turnoff or, if there isn't room, drive on to the East Portal of the Moffat Tunnel, about another mile. There are several railroad-track crossings to be aware of along the way.

Take FS 149 to the northeast and climb up out of the valley as it winds around toward the Rollins Pass summit, about 13 miles away. For the most part, the grade on this road is not that steep because it was once a railroad grade, and trains can only handle around a five percent–maximum grade. There are, however, several places where the road leaves the railroad grade and becomes quite a bit steeper.

Riding above treeline, and three miles yet to go to reach the summit of Rollins Pass!

The old grade is also very rough and in spots a bit technical. There are a couple of side trips that can be made on the east side of the pass, including Jenny Trail at about 10 miles from the portal, and Jenny Lake at about 12 miles.

The first part of the ride is through the aspen forest, then it leaves, if you will, and heads into the spruce and fir timber. Turning north, there is a great view of the plains, the foothills, Rollinsville, and the railroad below. As you climb past 10,000 feet, the wind becomes more crisp and the spruce and fir give way to pine and krummholz. You are very near tree line when you round the hairpin turn that wraps around Yankee Doodle Lake at about 10.5 miles. There can be snow through July on the road as you cross Jenny Creek, which is running out of Jenny Lake off to the right only .25-mile farther.

The rough road continues to climb at a gradual grade to the Forest Lakes trailhead at about 11,040 feet in elevation. Past this point there are snowfields that last most of the year and a gate, limiting traffic to foot, bicycle, and motorcycle. Traffic can be heavy before this point, because the road is good enough for two wheel drives, and motorcycles are common as well.

After Forest Lakes the road is completely above timberline and is closed to all motor vehicles, if not by the Forest Service, then by the boulders that have toppled down from road cuts above. At about 13 miles is the Needle Eye Tunnel, now closed to all with a large steel barricade. The trail climbs a precarious slope to the right and over the tunnel. Returning to the road on the other side you can ride the mile and a half to the summit of Rollins Pass. From the top of Rollins Pass, it is, of course, all downhill over the 17 miles to US 40 and then the final 2 miles to Winter Park. Again, this is the old railroad grade, so the grades are not too abusive. Remember how high the pass is if you decide to ride on down into Winter Park, and unless you are planning to stay over or refuel, it is not recommended that you try to ride the round-trip in one shot.

Riding down the west side of Rollins Pass or returning to the East Portal, or both, is a rough ride, and though you can make good time either way, it takes a good deal of concentration and skill. Let the bike float under you as much as possible, and watch for rocks, puddles, and minivans. This ride is also at high altitude, and your fitness has to be pretty good to deal with all of the factors associated with altitude. Remember that you get dehydrated a lot faster at higher altitudes, and that the sun is much more intense, especially with respect to ultraviolet radiation. Thus, always wear sunscreen, and two water bottles per cyclist are a must. All sorts of weather can be expected at any time of year, and when combined with a sudden snowstorm or rainstorm, the thin air, winds, and dropping afternoon sun can spell trouble. Take a jacket, and if you're riding later in the season (e.g., September), take along waterproof gear and equipment that will handle temperatures ten to twenty degrees lower than the temperature is at the beginning of the ride.

GOLDEN
area

*H*ome of the Colorado School of Mines and the less than picturesque—though economically important—Coors Beer plant, Golden is tucked behind North and South Table Mountains and at the mouth of Clear Creek Canyon. There are several good road-bike routes around Golden, including Lariat Loop Road, which climbs Lookout Mountain from the west end of town, and several mountain bike parks that provide miles of trail. It is rumored that if you ride long enough, you may even see Pete Coors out in the woods getting perspective.

Golden is named after Thomas Golden, who, along with James Saunders and George Andrew Jackson, started a mining camp there in 1858. Though Jackson made one of the first big gold strikes in Colorado, perhaps Golden had a more catchy last name.

Golden Gate Canyon State Park

Rating: Moderate to very difficult

Distance: 5–15 miles

Time required: 1–4 hours

Notes: Trails consist of smooth sand roads to bone-jarring rock-filled descents; campsites are available in the park; mountain biking is only allowed in the east (Jefferson Co.) side of the park; $3 fee

Quadrangles: Black Hawk, Ralston Buttes

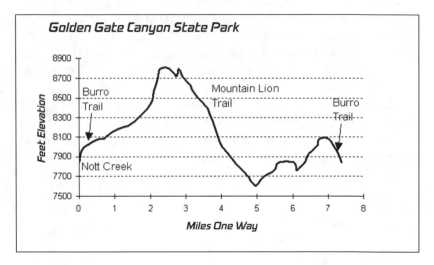

Golden Gate Canyon State Park is located northwest of Golden. The park is a picnic mecca, with more than two hundred picnic tables throughout the park and pit toilets at each parking area. The eastern side of the park (in Jefferson County) is the only part open to mountain bikes. The park offers many hiking trails, camping (both car and primitive sites), and panoramic views. The trails on the eastern side of the park range from moderate to very difficult. The moderate trails are mainly old sandy roads. The difficult trail sections include all of the steep rocky climbs to the top of

Golden Gate Canyon State Park (Eastern Half)

Elevation
Scale

9400ft
9300ft
9200ft
9100ft
9000ft
8900ft
8800ft
8700ft
8600ft
8500ft
8400ft
8300ft
8200ft
8100ft
8000ft
7900ft
7800ft
7700ft
7600ft
7500ft
7400ft
7300ft
7200ft

Trails:
1. Buffalo
2. Mountain Lion
3. Burro

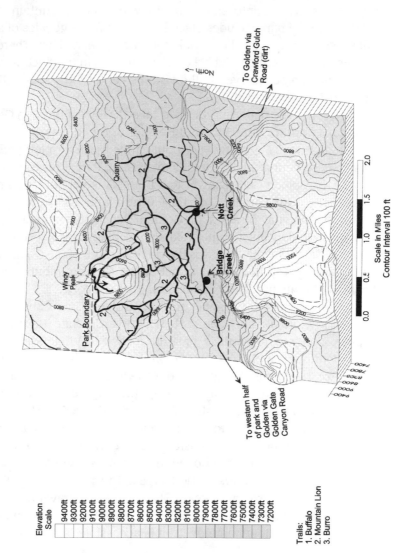

North →

To Golden via
Crawford Gulch
Road (dirt)

Nott Creek

Bridge Creek

Windy Peak

Park Boundary

Quarry

To western half
of park and
Golden via
Golden Gate
Canyon Road

Scale in Miles
Contour Interval 100 ft

0.0   0.5   1.0   1.5   2.0

Windy Peak and the very rocky and root-filled section of the Mountain Lion Trail along Deer Creek on the northern side of the park.

The landscape is composed of pine and aspen forest and grassy meadows nestled into small valleys with steep mountain sides. Wildlife in the park includes black bear (look for large piles of seed-filled scat), mountain lion (look for tracks), and deer. There are seven campsites and two backcountry shelters in this section of the park that can be reserved at the visitor's center (303/582-3707) for $2 and $10, respectively.

To reach the park from Denver, take US 6 west through Golden and turn north on SH 93 toward Boulder at the intersection of Colorado highways 6, 93, and 58. About 1 mile north turn left (west) at a sign designating Golden Gate Canyon State Park. This turn is onto SH 70, or Golden Gate Canyon Road. SH 93 is very busy, so make sure that you are completely in the left-turn lane. This turnoff is very near the original location of Golden Gate City, named not for Thomas Golden but for the gold mined in the hills to the west. Golden Gate Canyon Road was the original route of the Golden Gate and Gregory Toll Road used to get to the Gregory mining district, named after its first lucky prospector, John Gregory.

After 5 miles turn right (north) off Golden Gate Canyon Road onto Crawford Gulch Road (SH 57), toward White Ranch Open Space. Continue for 4 miles, past the turnoff to White Ranch Park, and continue on SH 57 for 5 more miles to the park's eastern entrance. If you miss the turnoff for Crawford Gulch Road, just keep going on Golden Gate Canyon Road, entering the park at the visitor's center and taking a right on to Ralston Creek Road.

If you plan to drive to the trailhead buy a $3 park pass at the self-service station at the eastern park entrance. Bikes are not required to pay if they are ridden into the park. Two areas may be used for parking. The first is Nott Creek. To reach Nott Creek after entering the eastern entrance on SH 57, take the gravel road about a mile into the park and turn right at the Nott Creek sign. The moderately difficult Mountain Lion Trail is accessible from this parking area.

The second parking area is 2 miles farther down SH 57 on the right at the Bridge Creek picnic area. From here, the difficult Burro

Riders of all shapes and sizes hit the trails at Golden Gate Canyon State Park.

Trail climbs out of the valley to an intersection with Mountain Lion Trail, 0.6-mile past Bridge Creek.

Mountain Lion Trail Loop: Moderate to difficult; 7.7 miles; 2—4 hours

The trails in the park can be ridden in a variety of ways. Here, the Mountain Lion Trail Loop is described, ridden clockwise. Other fun rides include the ride up Forgotten Valley and the challenging Burro Trail Loop, though the Mountain Lion Loop covers most of the trails in the park that are open to bikes.

Start by parking at the Bridge Creek picnic area. Follow the signs to Burro Trail and ride up the steep switchbacks for 0.6-mile to the intersection with Mountain Lion Trail. Take a left on Mountain Lion Trail. The trail climbs slowly up Nott Creek on a smooth sand road. At 0.8-mile, the turnoff to City Lights Ridge, an optional 0.5-mile side trip, takes off to the left. Continuing on Mountain Lion Trail, pass a small lake and abandoned cabin and ride on to mile 1.5, where the trail intersects the Buffalo Trail, which takes off to the left to Forgotten Valley. There are three primitive campsites and a backcountry shelter along Buffalo Trail. Continue on Mountain Lion Trail as it steepens considerably and climbs toward Windy Peak. The trail is steep but not terribly rocky.

After you complete the climb and enjoy a rolling stretch, Mountain Lion Trail reaches the Burro and Windy Peak Trails at 2.4 miles. Take a left, remaining on Mountain Lion Trail, or make a short side trip and climb .25-mile to the top of Windy Peak (9,100 feet in elevation). The Mountain Lion Trail descent is very rocky with a series of switchbacks followed by a very rocky and root-filled trail descending along Deer Creek. To avoid the rough Mountain Lion Trail descent, take the Burro Trail to the right and bear right, staying on Burro Trail to the parking area (2.3 miles from the top).

The Mountain Lion Trail descent passes another right turnoff to Burro Trail at 4.2 miles, then four campsites and a backcountry shelter in the next 0.5-mile. An unnamed 0.4-mile spur to a quarry branches to the left at 4.8 miles. The trail improves significantly as it follows an old road that drops into Deer Creek and back to the

Nott Creek parking area at 5.9 miles. Take a rest here, then get back on the Mountain Lion Trail and ride west for another moderately difficult 1.2 miles to Burro Trail. Turn left on Burro Trail and descend to the parking area to complete the 7.7-mile loop.

White Ranch Open Space Park

Rating: Moderate to very difficult

Distance: 5–15 miles

Time required: 1–4 hours

Notes: Lots of trails and lots of climbing

Quadrangles: Ralston Buttes

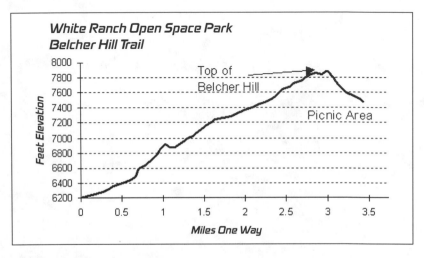

White Ranch Open Space Park
Belcher Hill Trail

Feet Elevation / Miles One Way

Top of Belcher Hill

Picnic Area

Named for the homestead ranch that was once perched atop the Front Range foothills, White Ranch Park is located just northwest of Golden. It can only be reached by SH 93, which connects Boulder and Golden, but there are two entrances, one on SH 93, and the other on Golden Gate Canyon Road (SH 70). We recommend using the east trailhead by taking the dirt road that tees in from the west about 3 miles north of Golden and US highway 6.

To reach this entrance, drive south from Boulder on SH 93 for about 15 miles, or north for 3 miles from Golden. Look for the White Ranch Park sign less than a mile south of the traffic light at the turnoff to Leyton. You can either park near SH 93 and ride the mile to the park or drive on to the ample parking lot at the trailhead.

To drive to the north of the mountain and ride from there, a

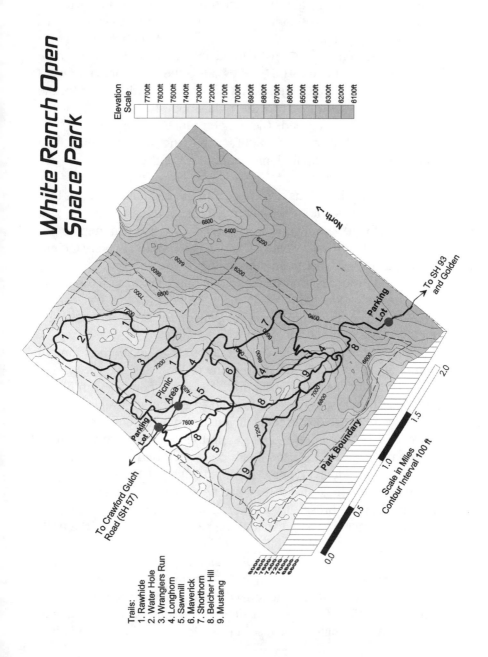

White Ranch Open Space Park

Elevation Scale

7700ft
7600ft
7500ft
7400ft
7300ft
7200ft
7100ft
7000ft
6900ft
6800ft
6700ft
6600ft
6500ft
6400ft
6300ft
6200ft
6100ft

North ←

To SH 93 and Golden

Parking Lot

To Crawford Gulch Road (SH 57)

Parking Lot

Picnic Area

Park Boundary

Scale in Miles
Contour Interval 100 ft

0.0   0.5   1.0   1.5   2.0

Trails:
1. Rawhide
2. Water Hole
3. Wranglers Run
4. Longhorn
5. Sawmill
6. Maverick
7. Shorthorn
8. Belcher Hill
9. Mustang

much easier outing, take the west turnoff from SH 93 on to the Golden Gate Canyon Road (SH 70), 1 mile north of Golden. This road will take you around the west side of White Ranch Park. Drive west on Golden Gate Canyon Road for about 4 miles to where Crawford Gulch Road (SH 57) takes off to the right (north) and SH 70 continues toward Golden Gate Canyon State Park. Watch for the White Ranch Park turnoff to the right about 4 miles north of the Golden Gate Canyon Road. The park entrance is 1.5 miles from this point. Both entrances have plenty of parking, a posted map, and pamphlets with a map and information. All of the trails in the park are marked with signs.

White Ranch Park as accessed from the east entrance is a hill-climber's paradise. It is recommended that you start from the east entrance if you want a good workout, because you will then be riding downhill on the way back. The ride is steep, rough, very technical in places, and just plain demanding. If you want an easier day out, drive to the west entrance and ride only the trails on top of the mountain (e.g., Rawhide and Wrangler). All of the other trails accumulate a good amount of elevation gain, on the order of 1,200 total feet from the east entrance.

There are some special considerations involved with mountain biking at White Ranch. Because many of the trails are very steep, there is limited visibility. This park is also very popular with hikers and equestrians, so remember to keep an eye out for trail traffic and control your speed on descents. If you are on a descent, please yield to other cyclists who are climbing up the grades, since you know how hard it is to get started again on a steep and technical climb. Of course, yield to everyone else, or at the very least yell out as you tumble down the trail so that people can stand clear until you bounce into the brush. If you experience a mishap and an injury, park personnel may be present at the picnic grounds or at the trailhead at the bottom of the hill.

At the east entrance, the main trail leading to the park from the parking area is the Belcher Hill Trail. This trail takes you up past the Golden Gun Club to a junction with the Maverick and Longhorn trails at 1.3 miles. (If you are sensitive to the sounds of war, you may want to don earplugs, because the Golden Gun Club range is just

Just some of the company you keep in the White Ranch Open Space Park.

over the hill, and it can get quite busy. Don't worry about stray bullets, however, because the range is well contained and on the other side of a small ridge.)

At this junction you must decide which route you want to take to get to the top. The Belcher Hill Trail climbs up from the southeast and provides access to the Mustang, Maverick, and Sawmill Trails, and the Longhorn Trail heads north from the Belcher Hill Trail, climbing and joining several other trails, including the Shorthorn and the north end of the Maverick Trail.

The Mustang Trail is crossed 1.8 miles from the trailhead, and it stays to the south and climbs steadily westward over sharp rocks up the deep Van Bibber Creek canyon, then joins the Sawmill Trail, which links back to the Belcher Hill Trail (a 0.6-mile cutoff) after 1.9 miles. The Mustang Trail rejoins the Belcher Hill Trail after another 0.4-mile. The west park entrance is a total of 2.6 miles from the junction.

The Mustang Trail is the width of a four-wheel-drive road,

which can be significant when you are trying to avoid large rocks or loose soil. After about a mile from the Belcher Trail the terrain turns into more of a rolling trail with intermittent climbs. This is a welcome sight to your legs but is short-lived because the climb up to the top is steep and technical.

The Belcher Hill Trail climbs up following a less technical fire-access road and provides some nice views of the plains. At 1.2 miles from the Mustang Trail junction the Belcher Hill Trail reaches a junction with the Sawmill connector (left/west) and the Maverick connector (right/east). On the Sawmill connector there is a rest room, drinking water, and a primitive campsite (available by permit only; inquire at the Open Space Park Office, 18301 W. 10th Ave., Golden). The Maverick connector leads to the Longhorn Trail after 0.9-mile and is more of a rolling trail, traversing the slope in many areas, and there are shady areas where snow can linger in the spring and fall. By continuing either on the Belcher Hill Trail for 1.1 miles or turning on the Maverick Trail to the Longhorn (a total of 1.6 miles), the picnic area and ranger station at the west entrance can be reached.

If you decide to take the Longhorn Trail, it is entirely single track and climbs and traverses the east side of the mountain. After 0.25-mile the junction with the Shorthorn Trail is reached. As the sign indicates, the Shorthorn is the left fork. It has stretches of smooth rolling trail but eventually turns west and climbs up. The Longhorn Trail drops down the side of the mountain, winding around to the north, then climbing back up to join the Shorthorn after 2.3 tough miles of narrow, dusty single track. The Shorthorn route is 1.8 miles and is much easier, though still difficult in its own right. After the Shorthorn and Longhorn trails rejoin, the Longhorn loops around to the west through the last climb for 0.5-mile to the junction with the Maverick. After 0.4-mile more the Longhorn splits at the picnic ground and tees into the Rawhide Trail at the rest rooms.

Once you navigate one or more of the trails to the top, there is a picnic ground with lots of people running around with plenty of blood sugar who obviously drove around to the west entrance and did not exhaust themselves as you have just done. This is okay, though, because you can yell that a bear chased you up the trail and collect enough potato salad for the ride back as they scamper for their minivans.

The Rawhide Trail forms a 4-mile loop around the top of the mountain. This loop is bisected by the Wranglers Run Trail and the 0.6-mile cutoff that goes to the Sourdough Springs Equestrian Camp (camping by permit only), a rest room, and drinking water.

Apex Park

Rating: Moderate to difficult

Distance: Apex Trail out and back, 5.5 miles; Grubstake Loop, 5 miles

Time required: 1–2 hours

Notes: Apex Trail is moderate, with climbs on the Grubstake Loop producing a difficult trail; great trail that is very close to Denver

Quadrangles: Evergreen, Morrison

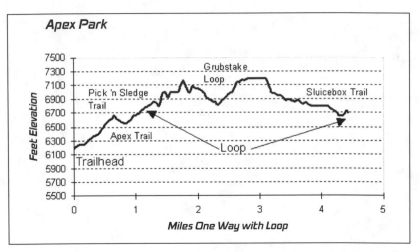

*A*pex Park is located in the southern part of Golden behind the Heritage Square amusement park and near the intersection of SH 93 and Colfax Avenue (US 40). Apex Park is named after the historic town of Apex. In the park, the Apex Trail follows a similar route to the old Apex and Gregory Toll Road, constructed in the 1860s. The road was a supply route that linked the town of Apex, located where the park now lies, to mining towns such as Central City in the hills. You can imagine having to hike up it with your grubstake, or trying to convince your mule that this is really what needs to be done. The original Apex and Gregory Toll Road route

Apex Park

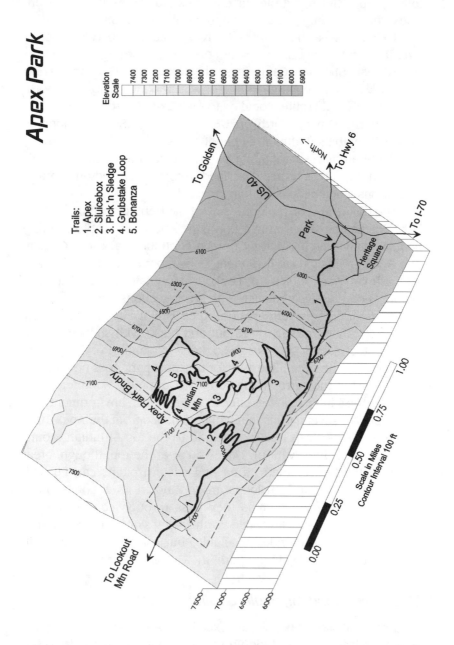

Trails:
1. Apex
2. Sluicebox
3. Pick 'n Sledge
4. Grubstake Loop
5. Bonanza

Elevation Scale

7400
7300
7200
7100
7000
6900
6800
6700
6600
6500
6400
6300
6200
6100
6000
5900

To Golden

US 40

North →

To Hwy 6

Park

Heritage Square

To I-70

To Lookout Mtn Road

Apex Park Bndry

Indian Mtn

Scale in Miles
Contour Interval 100 ft

0.00   0.25   0.50   0.75   1.00

follows Apex Gulch, but the current Apex Trail stops at the western Apex Park boundary just east of and parallel to CR 68.

To reach Apex Park from Denver, take US 40 (West Colfax Avenue) south from US 6 just south of Golden. Turn right at the Heritage Square Shopping Center (also the junction of US 40 and SH 93) and park in the shopping center's lower parking lot (on the north side). An alternate route would be to take Exit 259 from I-70 west to US 40 north. Driving north on US 40, Heritage Square Shopping Center is on the left after a couple of miles.

There are no rest rooms or picnic facilities at Apex Park. This park and the access routes described become crowded on summer afternoons when people are leaving work.

The trailhead is on the north side of the Heritage Square parking lot. Take the Apex Trail left (west) into the Apex Gulch (Apex is a very popular name here). The right branch continues back into Golden. The Apex Trail begins at 6,150 feet as a smooth, sandy single track that climbs Apex Gulch to Lookout Mountain Road. The trail becomes progressively rockier, with steep sections and logs placed across the trail to prevent erosion. Apex Trail itself is a moderately difficult 2.7-mile trail (5.4 miles out and back) with short technical sections that climbs 900 feet to Lookout Mountain Road. The trail stays close to the streambed and, for the most part, does not provide good views of the surrounding country. During the summer, however, the trees in the canyon offer a cool and lush environment.

There are several trails that can be reached from the Apex Trail. These require a steep,1,000-foot climb to the top of Indian Mountain (7,281 feet in elevation). Once you're at the top, though, great views of the Denver metro area and eastern plains can be had. There are trails that form loops around Indian Mountain and are smooth for the most part as they pass through contrasting dry south-facing slopes and wooded north-facing slopes. There are several combinations of rides available, but for this book we will describe the main loop in the park, the Grubstake Loop.

Grubstake Loop: Difficult; 5 miles, 1 – 2 hours

The Grubstake Loop is an excellent 5-mile trail for a quick workout close to town. Ride up the Apex Trail for 0.7-mile to the

Pick 'n Sledge Trail that takes off to the right (north). Take this right turn and begin climbing through switchbacks for 0.9-mile to over 6,800 feet in elevation and the junction with the Grubstake Loop. Take a right and begin the loop. The Pick 'n Sledge Trail, which continues to the left (it's less difficult after the climb) offers a quick 0.6-mile shortcut to Sluicebox Trail and a 0.3-mile descent back to Apex Trail, from which it is 1.4 miles to the parking area.

From the junction with the Pick 'n Sledge Trail, the Grubstake Loop Trail descends for 0.5 miles to where it meets the Bonanza Trail. The Bonanza Trail is a 0.3-mile, moderately difficult shortcut that bisects the Grubstake Loop by climbing over the top of the ridge. Bear right and continue on the Grubstake Loop, which offers a number of views of Denver and a smooth ride through the forest along Grubstake Gulch before climbing back to the top of Indian Mountain via several switchbacks.

The climb up the north side of Indian Mountain is difficult because of its steep grade, but the trail is smooth and the switchbacks are very rideable. One mile on the loop from the junction with the east end of the Bonanza Trail, you'll reach the west end of the Bonanza Trail shortcut. Continue to bear right and climb southwest toward Indian Mountain and the highest point on the loop. Only 0.2-mile south of the Bonanza Trail intersection the Grubstake Loop Trail ends at the Pick 'n Sledge Trail. From here you can take either the Pick 'n Sledge Trail (left) or Sluicebox Trail (right) back to the Apex Trail. For this description we will select the Sluicebox.

Take a right on Sluicebox Trail and descend the short, 0.3-mile descent through tight switchbacks to Apex Trail. The trail is fairly smooth, but a slip on a switchback could mean a nasty fall onto rock and cactus, typically requiring a good amount of duct tape to fix. Once you're at the Apex Trail take a left (east) and continue 0.7-mile back to the Pick 'n Sledge Trail junction, and then the final 0.7-mile back to the parking area. Caution should be exercised on the descent back down the Apex Trail due to the many people who will be riding and walking up the single track. Remember that all pedestrians and climbing cyclists have the right-of-way.

William Frederick Hayden Green Mountain Park

Rating: Moderate to difficult

Distance: 3–10 miles

Time required: 1–2 hours

Notes: Very rocky and steep single track

Quadrangles: Morrison

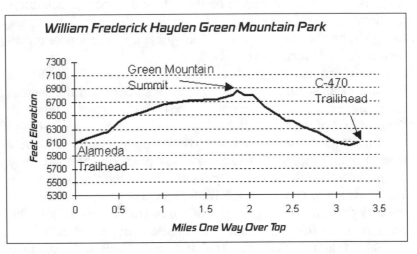

*T*his open space park is located on the western edge of the Denver metro area between the towns of Golden and Lakewood. The park is actually run by the town of Lakewood but is included here in the Golden group. The park is typically referred to simply as Green Mountain, though Mr. Green's full name was William Frederick Hayden Green (not to be confused with the former head of the U.S. Geological Survey in the late 1800s, Ferdinand V. Hayden). His family donated and sold land to the Lakewood parks system during the 1970s.

Green Mountain is a prominent physiographic landmark on the western side of the Denver metro area, just east of the Front Range

William Frederick Hayden
Green Mountain Park

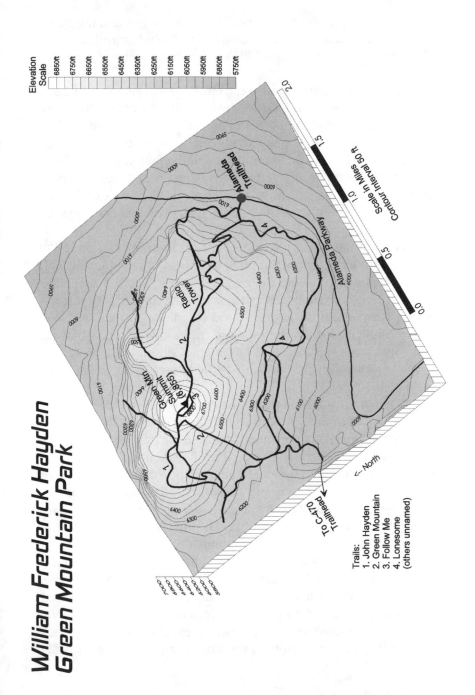

Elevation Scale

6850ft
6750ft
6650ft
6550ft
6450ft
6350ft
6250ft
6150ft
6050ft
5950ft
5850ft
5750ft

Alameda Trailhead

Alameda Parkway

Radio Tower

Green Mtn. Summit (6,855)

To C-470 Trailhead

← North

Scale in Miles
0.0   0.5   1.0   1.5   2.0

Contour Interval 50 ft

Trails:
1. John Hayden
2. Green Mountain
3. Follow Me
4. Lonesome
(others unnamed)

foothills in a transition zone between the mountains and the plains. It is an erosional remnant of river-deposited sand, gravel, and cobbles similar to the area around Rocky Flats and other surfaces along the range front.

To reach the park, head west on Alameda Parkway in Lakewood as it climbs around the south side of the mountain. There are a couple of trailheads along Alameda, and one on the west side of the park off C-470, on Rooney Road. The two most convenient trailheads are the Rooney Road trailhead and the first one that is found as you drive west on Alameda Parkway just past Green Mountain High School. The parking area is on the north (right) side of the road and the high school is on the south (left). For this book we will describe ride options starting at this trailhead.

To reach the Rooney Road trailhead from the south on C-470, take the exit to Morrison and drive into town, taking the first right turn that is marked as the route to Red Rocks Park and Amphitheater, SH 26. This road becomes Rooney Road once it gets past Red Rocks. Drive north on Rooney Road for about 2 miles, past Red Rocks Amphitheater on the left, and to the parking area that will come up on the right (east). It is the only parking area on Rooney Road—if you reach the left turn to Matthews/Winters Park, you have gone too far.

To reach the trailhead from the north, take the exit for Morrison and Red Rocks from I-70. Head south, past the turnoff to Matthews/Winters Park that comes up immediately on the right (west), and look for the parking area coming up on the left. Park and ride over C-470 on the overpass and to Green Mountain Park. You will come in right at the intersection of Lonesome Trail and Green Mountain Trail.

Green Mountain Park includes two single-track trails (Lonesome and John Hayden Trails) that skirt the park bottom and climb up onto the mountain. Green Mountain Trail is an unimproved road that climbs up the park's west side and traverses the crest (summit elevation 6,855 feet) for access to radio transmitters on top.

Several parts of trails and the road are described here, though this park is really a place to go and freelance, finding your favorite combination instead of taking routes prescribed by a guidebook. Most of the trails that climb up the sides of the mountain are quite

Scouting a route at the trailhead of the William Frederick Hayden Green Mountain Park.

steep and rocky, though not very technical, because the rocks are well rounded and usually not loose. There aren't any switchbacks, and Lonesome Trail, which skirts the south side of Green Mountain, is rolling with short climbs and can make for a good aerobic workout.

To begin a ride from the Alameda Parkway trailhead, park in the dirt parking lot and ride either east or west on Lonesome Trail. To the left (west), Lonesome Trail is more of a rolling trail that starts off with a very steep though short climb, then skirts the south side of Green Mountain with several unnamed trails that take off to the north and climb up the top. To the east, Lonesome Trail loops around the end of the mountain and immediately climbs up the east side. This climb is really a *burner* and a bit rough, but once you are up the steep grade the climb on across the top of Green Mountain is much easier, and you can choose where you want to drop back down. It would be best to ride all the way to the west side, past the summit, and then ride back around.

If you ride west from the parking lot, Lonesome Trail winds around and rolls through arroyos on the south side of Green Mountain. There are a couple unnamed trails that climb up ridges to the top of the mountain, and you may wish to explore them. Both are similar in required ability, with a rocky but not technical single track. If you ride completely around the west side of the mountain to the Green Mountain Trail (3 miles), there is a very steep climb just before the junction that will challenge you, though you can ride around it to the west and a road that leads up to the top, where there are radio towers (0.8-mile from the bottom to the junction with the John Hayden Trail and 1 mile to the Follow Me Trail and the summit). This dirt road is a really good workout and is rough and rocky in spots.

Once you're on top of Green Mountain, there are several different routes that will take you back down the east and south side to the trailhead, and to the John Hayden Trail, which drops off the north side of the mountain. There is also a small loop called the Follow Me Trail that circles around the summit.

Matthews/Winters Park and Hogback Park (Dakota Ridge)

Rating: Easy to very difficult

Distance: 1–10 miles

Time required: 30 minutes to 2 hours

Notes: Smooth sandy trails with optional steep/rocky climbs; can be very crowded on weekends

Quadrangles: Morrison

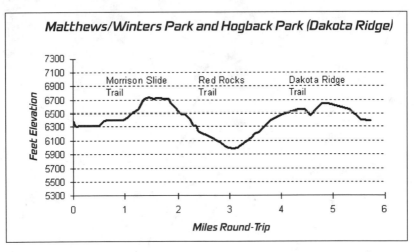

*T*o reach these parks from Denver, take I-70 west and exit onto SH 26 just before I-70 climbs into the foothills. Take SH 26 south toward Morrison and Red Rocks Park. A sign designates Matthews/Winters Park immediately on the right (west) side of SH 26. Park in the parking lot a short distance from the turnoff. Self-composting pit toilets, picnic tables, and shade trees are available at the trailhead.

Ride the Village Walk Trail to the south out of the parking area as it makes a 1-mile tour around the old town site of Mount Vernon. The actual ruins of the town are covered by a landfill near where SH

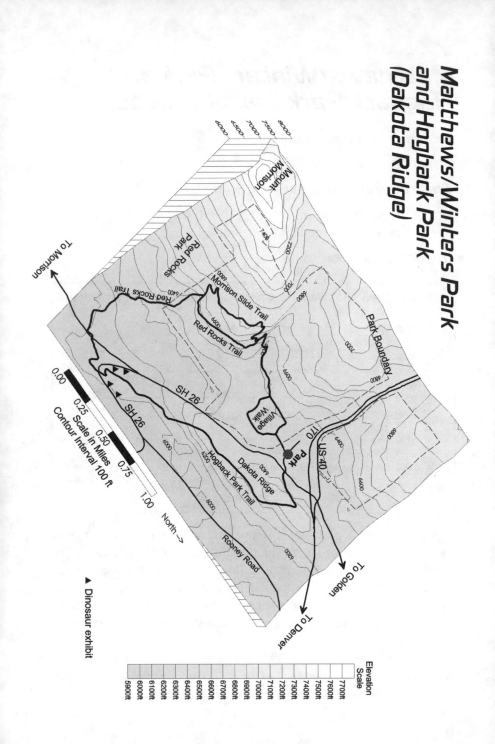

Matthews/Winters Park and Hogback Park (Dakota Ridge)

Mount Morrison

Red Rocks Park

Morrison Slide Trail

Red Rocks Trail

Red Rocks Trail

Village Walk

Park Boundary

SH 26

SH 26

Dakota Ridge

Hogback Park Trail

Rooney Road

To Morrison

To Golden

To Denver

I70

US 40

Park

North →

0.00 0.25 0.50 0.75 1.00
Scale in Miles
Contour Interval 100 ft

▲ Dinosaur exhibit

Elevation Scale

7700ft
7600ft
7500ft
7400ft
7300ft
7200ft
7100ft
7000ft
6900ft
6800ft
6700ft
6600ft
6500ft
6400ft
6300ft
6200ft
6100ft
6000ft
5900ft

93 passes under I-70. Mount Vernon was founded in 1859 by doctor and minister Joseph Casto. It was a supply town for mines to the west, similar to the other start-up towns in the area such as Apex and Golden Gate City. It is said that Casto grubstaked the famous prospector John Gregory when he was heading into the Central City area on his way to making his big strike.

The town of Mount Vernon became more than just a mining supply camp and actually had quite a storied history. Because Mount Vernon was founded seventeen years before Colorado acquired statehood, the area had no form of local government and there was little in the law-and-order line. So the people living there, though they numbered fewer than fifty, wanted some form of government. After voting down a traditional oligarchy, they decided to forgo the formalities that the United States Government required and form the Jefferson Territory and elect a governor. Because of the exposure it got during the mining days of the late 1850s, this new rogue territory may have had some influence on the timing of the formation of the Colorado Territory.

This territory was illegal in the eyes of the U.S. government, of course, but so were most of the claims made on the West, depending on who it was being claimed for. At any rate, the governor-elect was Judge Robert W. Steele. There is a monument in the park to Judge Steele that is located where his house once stood, and the old stone house of one of the inhabitants with a familiar last name, George Morrison, still stands.

Between 1859 and 1861 Mount Vernon was something of a political hub, acting as the local capital of sorts and as a gateway to the mining districts up Clear Creek. This heyday was short-lived, even though the Colorado Territory was created, for the most part, because of Mount Vernon. President Lincoln appointed his onetime bodyguard, William Gilpin, governor of Colorado Territory, and he moved the seat to Denver. Matthews/Winters Park is, in a way, a monument to the town of Mount Vernon and its influence on the early political history of Colorado, though little remains of the town site today.

Hogback Park contains Dakota Ridge, a geologic feature that was created by the tilting of beds of Dakota sandstone during the uplifting of the Front Range. The sedimentary beds exposed on Dakota Ridge are Cretaceous, which means they are from the age of the dinosaurs. And, as it turns out, there are dinosaur tracks and other trace fossils, such as disturbances in the form of very deep footprints where a very large dinosaur sank into the beds, which were at that time soft mud. These features are exposed, and there are interesting interpretive exhibits along SH 26 south of the entrance to Matthews/Winters Park as it crosses Dakota Ridge.

The trails in Matthews/Winters Park consist of smooth, sandy single track with optional steep technical sections on the Morrison Slide Trail and the Dakota Ridge. Two rides are described here. The first is a short, easy ride in Matthews/Winters Park, and the second is a longer loop that includes steep climbs and technical sections in both parks.

Red Rocks Trail: Easy to moderate; 3.9 miles, 25 minutes to 1 hour

This ride is an out-and-back ride on the Village Walk and Red Rocks Trails, with an option to include the more difficult Morrison Slide Trail. From the parking lot, ride south on the Village Walk Trail for 0.1-mile to the historic Mount Vernon town site. The trail at this point is very easy smooth sand. Take a right and ride 0.3-mile on Village Walk Trail to the moderately difficult Red Rocks Trail. Continue for 0.7-mile to the intersection with the Morrison Slide Trail. Stay left on the Red Rocks Trail and ride 0.8-mile to the junction with the other end of the Morrison Slide Trail. Ride back down the Red Rocks Trail, returning to the Village Walk Trail, and take the 0.6-mile right fork and the 0.1-mile trail back to the parking area. If you want to make the ride more of a challenge, take the difficult Morrison Slide Trail at the first intersection and climb 400 feet up switchbacks for a spectacular view. Continue on the Morrison Slide Trail, traversing the slope for a total of 1.2 miles from the first junction with the Red Rocks Trail to where the trails meet up again at the south end. From here, follow the Red Rocks Trail back to the north and the parking area via the Village Walk Trail.

A smooth start from the Matthews/Winters Park Trailhead.

Dakota Ridge and Red Rocks Loop: Difficult with steep climbs and rocky sections on Dakota Ridge; 6 miles, 1—2 hours

From the Matthews/Winters Park parking lot, ride back out the park entrance road to SH 26. Carefully cross the highway and ride up the Dakota Ridge Trail that climbs up directly ahead of you to Dakota Ridge in Hogback Park. The climb is a steep gravel road to the top of the ridge (.25-mile) where the Dakota Ridge Trail, marked with a sign, veers off to the right (south). From here the Dakota Ridge Trail follows the ridge crest to the south for 2 miles of rocky, sometimes very technical single track, all the way to where the hogback ends near Red Rocks Park. There are two short steep climbs over humps along the 2 miles of ridge.

Dakota Ridge is an excellent place to view eagles and hawks as they migrate and search for food through Colorado as well as the tracks of dinosaurs that lived here millions of years ago.

At the southern end of Dakota Ridge, the trail crosses Rooney Road. Continue to descend to where the Dakota Ridge Trail ends at SH 26. On the other (west) side of SH 26 is the beginning of the moderately difficult Red Rocks Trail. The next 0.8-mile stretch travels through Red Rocks Park, within view of the amphitheater—home of such classic concerts as U2's Under a Blood Red Sky and, recently, John Tesh's Live at Red Rocks. (Authors' note: We in no way endorse or condone listening to John Tesh music while cycling.) After leaving Red Rocks Park and returning to Matthews/Winters Park, the Red Rocks Trail turns west and climbs up a draw for 0.2-mile to the junction with the Morrison Slide Trail.

From the Red Rocks Trail–Morrison Slide Trail junction, you can take either trail. The Morrison Slide Trail is a 1.2-mile ride that climbs 200 feet through switchbacks before descending back down switchbacks to reconnect with the Red Rocks Trail. To avoid this climb, stay on the Red Rocks Trail to the right and ride the flat 0.8-mile to where the trails meet again.

From this second junction, take the Red Rocks Trail another easy 0.7-mile to Village Walk Trail, which splits and circumnavigates the Mount Vernon historic town site, with the left fork taking 0.3-mile and the right fork taking 0.6-mile. Take either fork and ride to where they join again, then ride the final 0.1-mile to the parking area.

IDAHO SPRINGS AND CENTRAL CITY *area*

*T*he Idaho Springs and Central City area is notorious in Colorado history for the large quantities of gold and silver that have been mined from beneath the hills. Like burrows in a prairie dog town, the scars of mines from days gone by are scattered through the area, numbering in the thousands. With the discovery of lode deposits of precious metals, all of the hullabaloo associated with the gold rush was alive in Denver-area towns, many of which are now no more than the remnants of foundations in the shrubs.

Today, the main east-west transportation route through Colorado is Interstate 70. As it leaves the Denver metro area, it passes through canyons once buzzing with gold fever and smoking smelters. I-70 has facilitated the growth of towns—bedroom communities for Denver in many cases—and ski resorts. It also provides access to many good mountain bike rides, from Idaho Springs all the way to Moab, Utah.

Many of the concerns that mountain bikers in Denver must face, most notably trail congestion, must now also be addressed when they travel west into the hills. I-70 is fairly open during the summer months for getting out of town, but the return trip at the end of the day can be grueling. Traffic can be slow-and-go from the Eisenhower Tunnel to Denver on a Sunday afternoon. This is not meant to deter you from doing rides accessed by I-70 but should serve as an advisory that at any time of year travelers on I-70 will preserve their sanity if they seek out alternative routes and schedule their return trips to miss the peak traffic hours.

Interstate 70 can be accessed from virtually every major thoroughfare in the Denver metro area. Interstate 25, Colorado 470, and U.S. Highway 6 are the main routes, and if you are coming from Boulder, SH 93 will bring you to I-70 via Golden. There are several good road rides along I-70, including the bike path from Frisco to Vail and road loops over Fremont, Tennessee, and Hoosier Passes. There are also other dirt-road rides such as those over Squaw and Guanella Passes. For the purpose of this guide, we have focused on rides that are fairly close to Denver. Several good rides are found between Idaho Springs and Central City, one of the most prolific mining areas in the Front Range, and in all of Colorado, for that matter.

Pisgah Lake Loop

Rating: Moderate

Distance: 8.4 miles round-trip

Time required: 1–2 hours

Notes: Four-wheel-drive road with views and moderate climbs to almost 9,700 feet

Quadrangles: Central City

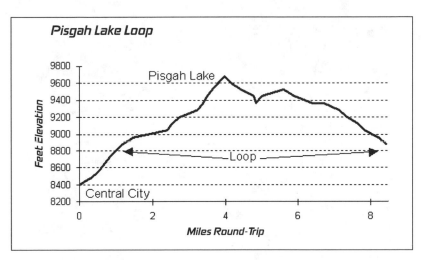

*P*isgah Lake is west of Central City and can be reached after riding over Oh My Gawd! Road if you are really ambitious. The Pisgah Lake trailhead is located near the historic mining town of Nevadaville, just west of Central City. Nevadaville was one of the towns that sprang up after the rush for gold that followed the first lode discovery in Colorado, by John Gregory in Prosser Gulch in 1859. Originally called Nevada City, the town was started in 1859 and soon grew larger than Central City or Black Hawk. The name Nevada City was changed to Bald Mountain because of mail delivery problems with Nevada City in California, but the townspeople were not happy with the change imposed by the postal service and continued to call the town Nevada City, causing further confusion

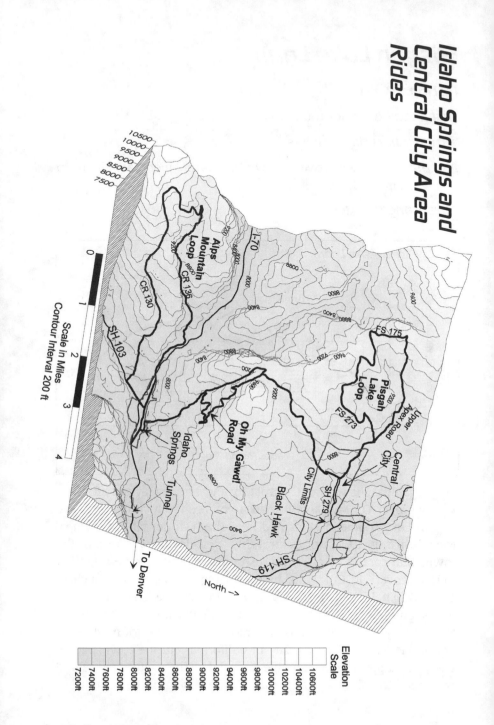

Idaho Springs and Central City Area Rides

Scale in Miles
Contour Interval 200 ft

Elevation Scale

7200ft
7400ft
7600ft
7800ft
8000ft
8200ft
8400ft
8600ft
8800ft
9000ft
9200ft
9400ft
9600ft
9800ft
10000ft
10200ft
10400ft
10600ft

Alps Mountain Loop CR 136
CR 130
SH 103
Pisgah Lake Loop
FS 175
Upper Apex Road
FS 273
Central City
City Limits
SH 279
Oh My Gawd Road
Idaho Springs Tunnel
Black Hawk
SH 119
I-70
To Denver
North →

with mail service. It was only after intervention by a visit by Post-master General Schuyler Colfax, who was at the time vying for the vice presidential nomination, that the dispute was settled. The townspeople opted for the name Nevadaville, though the post office name remained Bald Mountain.

Other interesting occurrences in Nevadaville were "Indian scares." Though it was against all odds and logic for Native Americans to attack an Anglo settlement, false rumors spread at least twice of an impending onslaught. This sent the townspeople into a panic. Once, a town drunkard found a Ute arrow and stuck it through his hat. He came riding into town claiming that the Utes were on the warpath, and everyone ran for cover. While the rest of the town was hiding, he drank his fill at the local saloon. The irony of the situation is not that the threat of Ute attacks did not exist, but that a man in Central City heard of the prank and it worked for him as well.

These false alarms were unfortunate, because another such case had prompted military action against Utes in the area by the self-designated "protector of Colorado," Major J. M. Chivington of the Sand Creek Massacre infamy.

Some of the biggest mineral strikes in the rich area were discovered in nearby Nevada Gulch just after Gregory's strike in Prosser Gulch in 1859. Eight working mines were located in Nevada Gulch, and this prosperity led to a bustling and booming downtown Nevadaville throughout the 1870s, 1880s, and 1890s that survived five different fires, each of which nearly wiped out the town. There are still remnants of the town that have not been vandalized, so if you decide to explore the town site, please take only pictures.

The description here is for riding a counterclockwise loop past Columbine Campground, up to Pisgah Lake, and back down.

To reach Central City from Denver, take I-70 west for about 15 miles to Exit 244, the turnoff to US 6. Follow the signs to Central City that will direct you west on US 6 for 3 miles to the junction with SH 119. Take a left on 119 at the stoplight and head north. From here it is about 8 miles to the left turn on SH 279, which runs through Black Hawk and Central City. Drive through Black Hawk and start looking for a place to park. This may not be easy due to the gambling operations in the town, and you may have to drive on through or pay for a spot at one of the lots built on old mine tailings.

Ride west out of Central City on the continuation of SH 279 (also known as the Upper Apex Road) for 1 mile to the junction with FS 176. Do not take 176, but bear right on Upper Apex Road to Columbine Campground. Note that FS 273, which takes off to the south here, is your return route. The beginning of the loop is already at about 9,000 feet in elevation, but there isn't much climbing for the first 1.5 miles to Columbine Campground. Just before Columbine Campground you'll see the turnoff to the left for Pisgah Lake Road, but don't take it. Keep going straight, and climb steadily to the junction with FS 175 at mile 2.6 (almost 9,700 feet in elevation). From here it is all downhill and about 3 miles to the end of the loop. Ride south on FS 175 for 1 mile, past several junctions with other unimproved roads and old mines, to the junction with FS 273. Bear left on FS 273 and follow the gradual drop back down for about 2 miles to a turnoff to the old town site of Nevadaville. If you wish to check out the old mines and ruins, use caution, because the structures and slopes can be unstable and dangerous. And, of course, avoid any open excavations such as adits (entrances to underground mine workings). Ride down FS 273 for another mile across Eureka Gulch and to the junction with FS 176. Turn right on 176 and ride back into Central City. By now, the guys from the Central City casino to whom you owe money may have lost your trail.

Oh My Gawd! Road (see map, p. 132)

Rating: Moderate to difficult

Distance: 16 miles to Central City and back

Time required: 2–4 hours

Notes: Smooth historic road, but continuous climb above 8,000 feet elevation

Quadrangles: Idaho Springs, Central City, Black Hawk

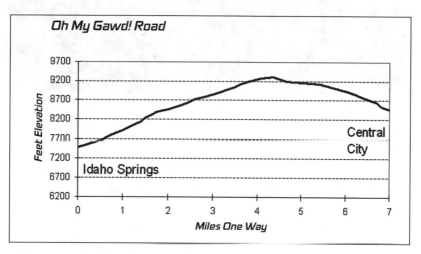

Oh My Gawd! Road

I f you are looking for a good, smooth, consistent climb at moderate altitude, try the Oh My Gawd! Road (also known as the Oh My Gosh! or Oh My God! Road).

The Oh My Gawd! Road (CR 279) was constructed in the 1870s to support mines in the hills above Idaho Springs and over the hill to the north at Central City. The road grade is about seven percent, the maximum that the old ore wagons, and now large trucks and machinery, can take. A common workout is to ride up Oh My Gawd! Road and over the ridge separating Idaho Springs from Central City, then to drop into Central City. Once in Central City you can see the town and maybe get something to eat, then ride back over the mountain to Idaho Springs. Two or three times over and back, and

Mine spoils along Oh My Gawd! Road

you'll be in pretty good shape! But be careful gambling in Central City: Never bet more than you can afford to lose, which includes your wheels.

During the heavy summer tourist season you'll share the Oh My Gawd! Road with gamblers, weekend motorists, and truck traffic, but the visibility is good, even around the many hairpin turns. On the downhill you may end up overtaking that Mercury with Kansas plates, but be careful and wait for it to pull over to let you pass, because, as the driver's knuckles will attest, it's a long way down.

To reach the Oh My Gawd! Road from Denver, drive west on I-70 for about 20 miles to Idaho Springs. Take the first exit (241) off I-70 to Idaho Springs and drive down Colorado Boulevard and the strip of diners and motels to the small city park on the right at the corner of Colorado Boulevard and 23rd Street. Park at the city park and begin the ride, turning right on 23rd Street. Ride for a couple blocks, past Riverside Drive to Virginia Avenue. Turn left and ride for .25-mile to the first stop sign and turn right. You are now on Oh My Gawd! Road. Reset your odometer, as trip mileage will start here.

As you leave the edge of town and begin climbing up Virginia Canyon, the pavement ends and an improved gravel surface begins. There are two routes you can take up Virginia Canyon, and a couple of side trips. You can opt for a tour of local mines, for looping back to Idaho Springs, or you can ride on over to Central City.

A detailed and informative narrative of a tour on Oh My Gawd! Road was published by Pat Mosch in the small local newspaper *The Virginia Canyon Prospector* in the summer of 1996. It's available at the visitor information center located just west of the city park in Idaho Springs, on the south side of the street, and some of the historical information in this description is taken from this source.

At about 0.5-mile you will reach a fork in the road with several large signs on the left fork announcing "Road Closed." The left fork is not named. Take a right and head back to the south, still climbing. As you ride, listen and look for cars, of course, but also make a mental note of washboards in the road, because they will be a problem on the way back down. The road winds, traversing the slope and climbing steadily for another 2 miles past old mine workings, many from the late 1800s, until it finally rejoins the closed road that you left at the fork. Bear right at this intersection and ride on up the grade.

At about 3 miles in a gulch on the right you'll see the Idaho Tunnel and the portals to the Kangaroo and Metropolitan Mines. These mines were first operated in the 1870s and combined to produce over 2,000 feet of tunnels. You will pass a hole in the ground on the left at about 3.1 miles where a mine collapsed, eating its way all the way up to the ground surface, forming a sinkhole. Features like this are all too common in mining country, so stay away from any mine opening, for obvious reasons.

At about 4 miles there is a turnoff to the right for an unnamed road that leads to the historic location of Gilson Gulch. This side trip is a little over a half mile up to the site. Nothing remains of the town except for some old tailings piles, for much of the site has been covered by more recent mining operations. The Gilson family established the town in the 1870s, and by the 1890s it boasted a boardinghouse, saloon, grocery, and general store, and was supplied predominantly by wagon freight from Idaho Springs.

You'll pass several other workings along the way up the Oh My Gawd! Road, including the Comstock Mine at about 6 miles, which produced over $200,000 in gold and silver. The mine has recently been reopened, as evidenced by the new orange head frame over the portal.

At about 7 miles you will reach the top of the pass and a junction with another unnamed road. To the left (west) is a loop back to Virginia Canyon, and straight ahead (north) is the long downhill to Central City and Black Hawk. Take a look back south at Mount Evans and the canyon below where you started. Look at the sky for a weather update, check your legs, and decide which way you want to go. Remember that you will have to ride back over this pass from Central City if you decide to ride on.

On the way to Central City you will pass several modern and historic mining operations and may encounter quite a bit of car traffic, but the descent is quick and easy, with some opportunity for high speeds. Head on down into Central City and take a breather, and decide whether you want to ride on back to Idaho Springs or try the side trip to Pisgah Lake described in the previous section.

On the ride back to Idaho Springs, take the same route on Oh My Gawd! Road. There are other unnamed roads mentioned previously that lead to mines on the slopes above Idaho Springs, but we recommend that you stay on the main Oh My Gawd! Road route that has been described.

Alps Mountain Loop *(see map, p. 132)*

Rating: Moderate to difficult

Distance: 10.5 miles round-trip

Time required: 2 hours

Notes: Good climbs up a dirt road, lots of old mines

Quadrangles: Idaho Springs

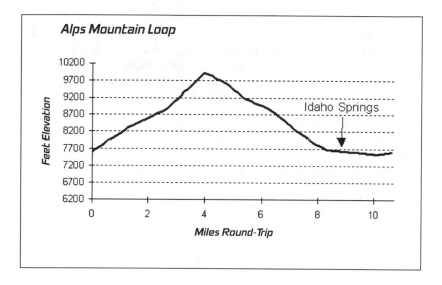

South of Idaho Springs is another area where mining operations have gone crazy during the last century. Mines just across Clear Creek from Idaho Springs were extracting ore from several rich lode deposits that are part of the same geologic setting as the mines between Idaho Springs and the Central City/Black Hawk area.

Drive west to Idaho Springs from Denver on I-70, taking the second Idaho Springs exit (240). This is the exit for SH 103 and SH 5 to Echo Lake and Mount Evans (Mount Evans is a fee area, $6 per carload; bikes enter free), both of which offer challenging road-bike rides. Turn left and head up SH 103 to the south and park at a parking lot on the left just across the bridge over Clear Creek. This is the start and end of the loop. Ride south on SH 103 for about 0.5-mile to a turnoff to the right on CR 130 (also known as Spring Gulch Road). Ride west on CR 130, which winds and climbs through literally hundreds of old prospects and producing mines that were started during the gold rush of the 1860s and thereafter. Colorado Road 130 follows Spring Creek for 4.6 miles to the foot of Alps Mountain, then turns to the north and winds around before dropping down along Trail Creek toward I-70. Where the road turns north and begins dropping it becomes CR 136, known as Trail Creek Road.

At the bottom of the grade you will reach a junction with CR 132 to the left (west) and an unnamed frontage road along I-70 that takes off to the right. Turn right on the frontage road and follow Clear Creek back toward Idaho Springs for 1 mile to where it turns north and passes under I-70. This will take you to the north end of Colorado Boulevard in Idaho Springs. Turn right into Idaho Springs and ride for 0.9-mile down Colorado Boulevard through the narrow town to the marked turnoff to SH 103 at 13th Street. Turn right again and ride back across I-70 to the start of the loop.

EVERGREEN
area

Southwest of Denver, the town of Evergreen and the surrounding area has grown rapidly over the last ten years and has seen highway and subdivision building that give it the conveniences of other Denver suburbs. It is cooler because of its higher elevation, and there is some good riding around the town. Every year the town hosts the Evergreen Triathlon, and the Team Evergreen Cycling Club sponsors events like the Triple Bypass, an organized noncompetitive road-bike ride over three mountain passes.

Elk Meadow Park

Rating: Easy to difficult

Distance: 1–10 miles

Time required: 1–4 hours

Notes: Smooth sandy trails with optional steep climbs and views of meadows and the eastern plains

Quadrangles: Squaw Pass, Evergreen

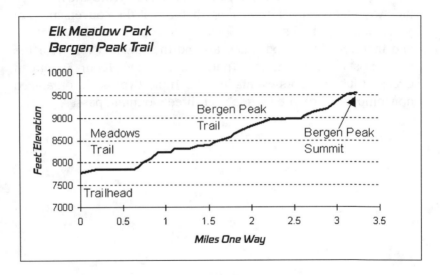

*E*lk Meadow Park consists of a vast meadow on the lower east side and challenging hills to the west. This is the home of such animals as the Richardson ground squirrel, pocket gopher, badger, and deer. The meadow region is also home to many wildflowers, grasses, and birds. As you climb the hills to the west of the park, the rise in elevation takes you from the transitional to the foothills ecosystem, then to the montane, and finally to the subalpine ecosystem at the top of Bergen Peak. Animals common in the transitional ecosystem are the Abert's squirrel (a large black squirrel

Elk Meadow Park

Trails:
1. Bergen Peak Trail
2. Too Long Trail
3. Meadow View Trail
4. Elkridge Trail
5. Painters Pause Trail
6. Sleepy "S"

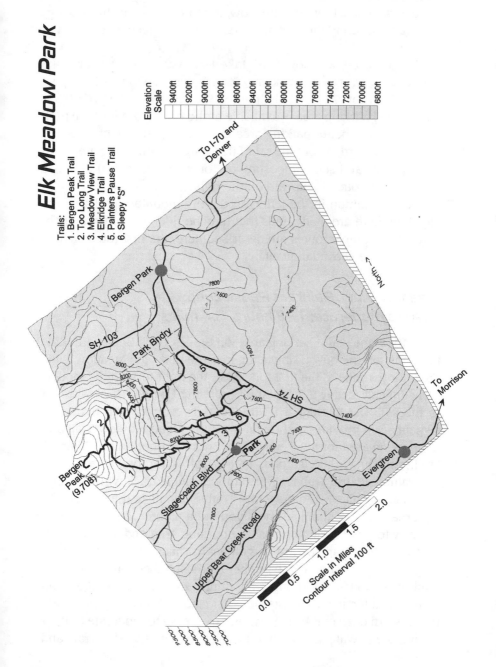

Elevation Scale

9400ft
9200ft
9000ft
8800ft
8600ft
8400ft
8200ft
8000ft
7800ft
7600ft
7400ft
7200ft
7000ft
6800ft

To I-70 and Denver

Bergen Park

SH 103

Park Bndry

Bergen Peak (9,708)

Stagecoach Blvd

Upper Bear Creek Road

Park

SH 74

Evergreen

To Morrison

North →

Scale in Miles
Contour Interval 100 ft
0.0   0.5   1.0   1.5   2.0

with tasseled ears), deer, and elk. The trees consist of scattered ponderosa pines. From the meadow, the forest changes from Douglas fir and aspen in the foothills ecosystem to lodgepole pine in the montane.

To get to Elk Meadow Park, take I-70 west from Denver. Take Exit 252 to Evergreen Parkway/SH 74 East. Follow SH 74 past Bergen Park for .75-mile. The park is visible to the west of SH 74, and a small parking area is available at the north corner of the park along SH 74 (a better parking area lies ahead). Turn right on Stage Coach Boulevard, before the set of traffic lights. A parking area with picnic tables and self-composting pit toilets is available 1.25 miles down Stage Coach Boulevard on the right.

As is common in the Jefferson County mountain parks, at Elk Meadow there are many trails that may be ridden in any variety of ways. Two sample routes are described here, the first rated easy to moderate, the second difficult.

Meadow View/Painters Pause Loop: Easy to moderate; 1–2 hours, 5.4 miles

Park at the south parking area, off Stage Coach Boulevard. Ride northeast on the only trail leading into the park, the Meadow View Trail, for 0.3-mile to the first fork. Take the right fork on the moderately difficult Sleepy S Trail. At 0.9-mile the Elkridge Trail takes off to the left. The Elkridge Trail (moderately difficult with two short switchbacks) provides a shortcut back the Meadow View Trail and the parking area for a 2.5-mile loop. But bear right on the Sleepy S Trail to the junction of Painters Pause Trail at 1.4 total miles.

Painters Pause Trail is a very smooth single track with little elevation gain. Follow Painters Pause Trail for a mile to the north parking area at 2.4 total miles, and if you are a painter, do pause along the way to reflect. Ride on past the parking area and take a left on Meadow View Trail, toward Bergen Peak. This section of the trail is easy, with only a short climb just before the intersection of Too Long Trail at 3.3 miles. Too Long Trail climbs 2.4 miles toward Bergen Peak over difficult terrain. Stay left on Meadow View Trail as it skirts the western edge of Elk Meadow along an easy to moderate trail. At 4.3 miles you will pass another intersection with Elkridge Trail, and

The mellow Meadow View Trail at Elk Meadow Park.

at 4.5 miles an intersection with Bergen Peak Trail (difficult). Bear right, staying on the Meadow View Trail, and ride back to the parking area at 5.4 total miles.

Bergen Peak Loop: Difficult; 2–4 hours, 10.1 miles

This route climbs steeply from the beginning at 7,750 feet in elevation up a rough trail to the top of Bergen Peak at 9,708 feet. This loop can be ridden either way—we picked the counterclockwise direction due to a personal preference for quick descents. To be specific, we prefer to start on the easy to moderate Meadow View Trail when our legs are fresh, then to climb the more technical and switchback-laden Too Long Trail, then to descend on the less technical Bergen Peak Trail. Try both directions on different days and decide what you like.

Park at the south parking area, off Stage Coach Boulevard. Take the Meadow View Trail for 0.3-mile to the junction with the Sleepy S Trail. Stay left on Meadow View Trail and ride west for 2.4 miles, passing turnoffs for the Bergen Peak Trail at 0.9 total miles and the

Elkridge Trail at 1.1 total miles. Meadow View Trail becomes easier, continuing for another mile to the intersection with Too Long Trail from the left at 2.7 total miles. This is where the difficult climbing begins.

Take a left and ride west on Too Long Trail. The trail climbs up over rough, rocky trail through difficult switchbacks for a grueling 2.4 miles—almost too long. At 4.5 total miles you are almost to the top, reaching the junction with Bergen Peak Trail. From here you can climb to the top of Bergen Peak by taking a right, or continue on straight ahead to finish the loop.

Turn right and climb through steep switchbacks over the final 1 mile and 500 vertical feet to the top of Bergen Peak. Note the weather conditions and your leg conditions. Lightning storms can build quickly, and because Bergen Peak is the highest point in the area, a fast descent may be required. From the summit of Bergen Peak there are great views of the Front Range to the north, west, and south, and of the foothills, Evergreen, and Bergen Park to the east.

Descend back down from Bergen Peak, and at the intersection of the Bergen Peak and Too Long Trails, take the Bergen Peak Trail to the right. This is a fast descent with a few switchbacks and some loose rock until you reach the Meadow View Trail at 9.2 miles. Take a right on Meadow View and return to the parking area at 10.1 total round-trip miles.

Mount Falcon Park

Rating: Easy to difficult depending on which ride is selected

Distance: 1–10 miles

Time required: 1–4 hours

Notes: Smooth sandy trails with optional steep climbs and views
of meadows and the eastern plains

Quadrangles: Morrison

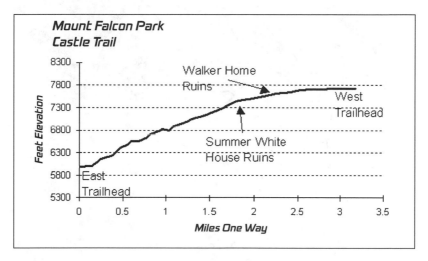

Mount Falcon Park is located 1 mile southwest of Morrison on SH 8. There are parking areas on the west (at the base of Mount Falcon) and the east (at the top of Mount Falcon) side of the park. Both parking areas are equipped with self-composting toilets, and the east side has a picnic area and a water pump. To reach Mount Falcon Park, take Hampden Avenue (US 285) west from Denver for about 5 miles to the Morrison/SH 8 exit. This exit will take you to the east park entrance. Turn right on SH 8 and drive for 2 miles to Forest Avenue, which takes off to the left (west). This turn is marked by a Mount Falcon Park sign. Turn left (west) on Forest Avenue and drive for 0.2-mile, then take a right on Vine Street. The parking area is another .25-mile ahead.

Mount Falcon Park

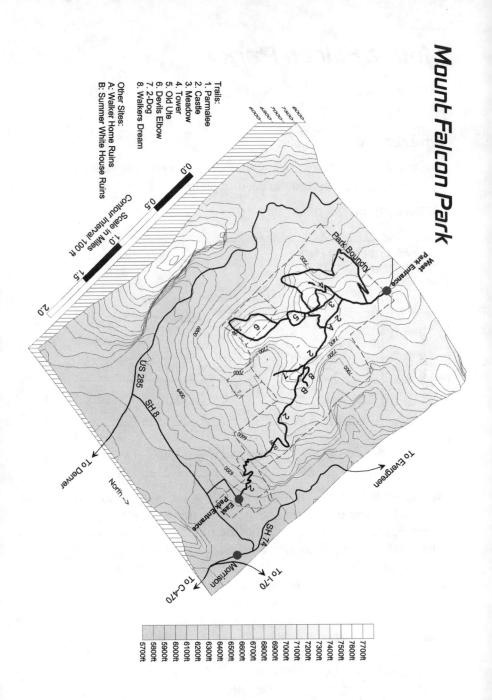

Trails:
1. Parmalee
2. Castle
3. Meadow
4. Tower
5. Old Ute
6. Devils Elbow
7. 2-Dog
8. Walkers Dream

Other Sites:
A: Walker Home Ruins
B: Summer White House Ruins

Scale in Miles
Contour Interval 100 ft.

0.0 0.5 1.0 1.5 2.0

North →

To Denver
To C-470
Morrison
To I-70
To Evergreen
East Park Entrance
West Park Entrance
Park Boundry
US 285
SH 8
SH 74

5700ft 5800ft 5900ft 6000ft 6100ft 6200ft 6300ft 6400ft 6500ft 6600ft 6700ft 6800ft 6900ft 7000ft 7100ft 7200ft 7300ft 7400ft 7500ft 7600ft 7700ft

To reach the west entrance to Mount Falcon Park, continue on US 285 past the SH 8 exit for another 2.5 miles to the Parmalee Gulch Road (CR120)/Indian Hills exit. Take this exit and drive northwest for 4.5 miles to the marked turnoff to the right on Picutis Road. This road winds around, turns into Comanche Road, then meets Nambe Road. Turn right (east) on Nambe Road and head into Mount Falcon Park. The total distance from Parmalee Gulch Road to the park entrance is 1.8 miles.

The east and west entrances are at different elevations, thus offering different amounts of climbing. The western parking area starts the ride directly at the top of the ridge at rolling meadows with little climbing. This is a good place to start if you are interested in good views without a difficult climb. The east entrance (6,000 feet in elevation) services a steep 2.7-mile climb to the top of Mt. Falcon (7,600 feet in elevation).

Mount Falcon Park is dedicated to the legacy of John Brisben Walker, who owned over 4,000 acres in the area during the early 1900s. He came out from West Virginia, where he made a fortune on land speculation and as owner of *Cosmopolitan* magazine, though the cover photographs were a bit different then. He also bought the Stanley Steamer Company (see p.38) but lost big on that one, as you don't see any Steamers on the highways these days. At the time Walker bought the company it was competing with Ford.

Walker bought Colorado land and had plans to build a resort, which he called the Summer White House, that would be a summer home for U.S. presidents. He built an elaborate stone house on Mount Falcon, which he lived in until it burned in 1918. His plans for the Summer White House never got further than the laying of the cornerstone because of financial troubles. Walker's luck never turned around and he died a poor man in 1931, but evidence of his brief life in the aristocracy is visible at Mount Falcon Park. Trails take you past the Walker home ruins and the Summer White House site.

The route described here includes the steep climb up Castle Trail from the west side of the park to the Summer White House site and the Walker home ruins.

Historic castle ruins at Mount Falcon Park.

Park at the east park entrance. Ride west on Castle Trail, which climbs 1,400 vertical feet to the top of Mount Falcon over 2.7 miles. The trail is long and steep with switchbacks, erosion-control devices, and loose rock but is not terribly technical. At the junction marked with a sign for Walkers Dream and Summer House, turn right and climb to an elevation of 7,613 feet over 0.4-mile of moderately difficult trail to the site of Walker's proposed Summer White House. Good views of Red Rocks Park and Denver are had from this point.

Ride back down to the Castle Trail for a total of 3.5 miles. At this junction you can take an easy 0.2-mile side trip on 2-Dog Trail. Turn right and continue on the Castle Trail as it becomes an easy ride, rolling over a meadow to the Walker home ruins 0.5-mile later at the junction with the Meadow Trail. The Walker home ruins are all that remains of Walker's mansion after it burned in 1918, and the site is fragile, so please stay off it.

From the ruins, several small loops can be ridden. None of the trails are difficult except the Tower Trail, which climbs about 200 feet to 7,851 feet in elevation. The remainder of the Castle Trail (0.7-mile to the western parking area) is easy, as is the Meadow Trail (0.6-mile). Other possible loops include the Parmalee Trail (2 miles), Old Ute Trail (0.4-mile), and Devil's Elbow Loop (1.1 mile). These are all moderately difficult and begin from the Meadow or Castle Trails. Whichever loop you choose, you will have to return to the east parking area via the Castle Trail.

Depending upon weather and energy levels, ride any or all of these trails. Return by riding back down Castle Trail through the meadow and descend down the mountain to the parking area for a total of 7.2 miles.

Alderfer/Three Sisters Park

Rating: Easy to difficult; two loops are described

Distance: 1–10 miles

Time required: 1–2 hours

Notes: Views of meadows, rock outcrops, and surrounding mountains

Quadrangles: Evergreen, Conifer

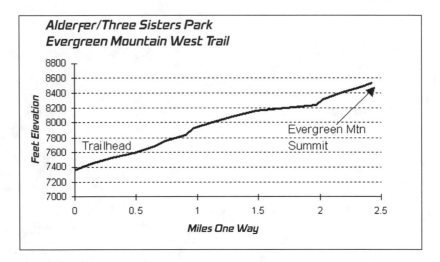

**Alderfer/Three Sisters Park
Evergreen Mountain West Trail**

To get to Alderfer/Three Sisters Park, take I-70 west from Denver. Take Exit 252, to Evergreen Parkway/SH 74 east. Follow SH 74 for 7.5 miles past Bergen Park and south to Evergreen. At the first stoplight past Evergreen Lake and at the beginning of town, take a right on SH 73. Proceed south on 73 out of town for 0.5-mile and take a right (west) on South Buffalo Park Road. Pass Evergreen High school and houses scattered through the hills and drive about 1.5 miles to the park. There are two park entrances and parking areas in the park. The first is located at the eastern edge, on the right (north) side of South Buffalo Park Road. The second is on the western side of the park, also on the north side of South Buffalo

Alderfer/Three Sisters Park

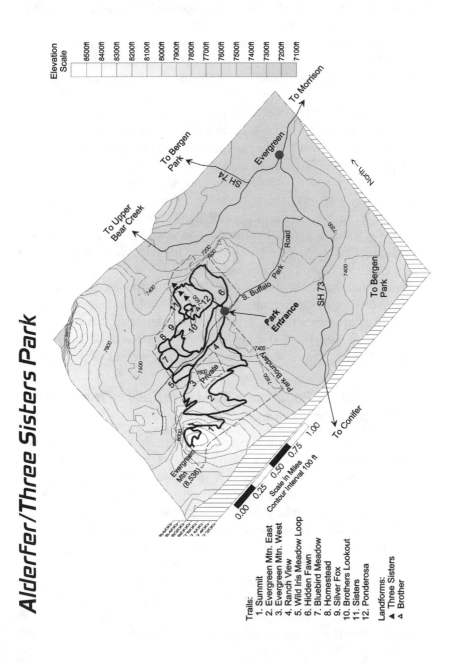

Elevation Scale

8500ft
8400ft
8300ft
8200ft
8100ft
8000ft
7900ft
7800ft
7700ft
7600ft
7500ft
7400ft
7300ft
7200ft
7100ft

To Morrison

To Bergen Park

SH 74

Evergreen

To Upper Bear Creek

7200

7400

7800

7600

S. Buffalo Park Road

Park Entrance

SH 73

7200

7400

To Bergen Park

North

7400

Park Boundary

7400

7800 Private

7600

7600

8000

Evergreen Mtn. (8,536')

8,800
8,000
8,000
7,800
> 7,600
> 7,400
> 7,200

0.00 0.25 0.50 0.75 1.00

Scale In Miles

Contour Interval 100 ft

Trails:
1. Summit
2. Evergreen Mtn. East
3. Evergreen Mtn. West
4. Ranch View
5. Wild Iris Meadow Loop
6. Hidden Fawn
7. Bluebird Meadow
8. Homestead
9. Silver Fox
10. Brothers Lookout
11. Sisters
12. Ponderosa

Landforms:
▲ Three Sisters
▲ Brother

To Conifer

Park Road. The second area has pit toilets, picnic areas, and the historic Alderfer homestead, built in 1894.

The Three Sisters are rock masses that have some historical significance because they were used as landmarks by early homesteaders in the area. They are erosional remnants of quartz-rich metamorphic rock that is common to the area.

E. J. and Arleta Alderfer bought the ranch that now makes up part of the park in 1945 and moved into the old ranch house, which had been built by a rancher named George Dollison in 1894. James Hester built the original homestead in 1873, but it burned in 1894. The Alderfers raised silver foxes and Aberdeen cattle until 1970, when they began running horses on the land. They bought and leased more and more land until their spread totaled more than 1,000 acres. The Alderfers gratefully donated the land in the park to Jefferson County. The northern parts of the park were obtained from the Spencer Wyant family. As you drive through the suburban sprawl that was once mountain forest, thank these families and the Jefferson County Open Space Parks for the trails you have to ride on.

The park has a number of trails that can be ridden in any variety of ways. Two loops will be described here that cover many of the trails. The first loop is easy to moderate, the second loop is difficult.

Hidden Fawn/Ponderosa Trail Loop: Easy to moderate; 30 minutes to 1 hour, 3.1 miles

Park at the east entrance and ride north (away from South Buffalo Park Road) out of the parking area. You will immediately reach the Hidden Fawn Trail, on which you should turn right. From here the trail is an easy ride around the northeast corner of the park and meets the Sisters Trail at 0.7-mile. Stay left on Hidden Fawn Trail instead of taking the difficult 0.7-mile climb through the Three Sisters rock outcrops on the Sisters Trail to the right.

Follow Hidden Fawn Trail to the intersection with Ponderosa Trail, to the right at 1 total mile. Continue on the moderately difficult Ponderosa Trail as it climbs toward the Brother rock outcrop. At 1.3 miles, pass the Brother Overlook Trail, an 0.2-mile spur to the top of the Brother that takes off to the right. The Brother Overlook Trail is

The top of Mount Evergreen is a perfect place to rest in Alderfer/ Three Sisters Park.

difficult but offers views of the Three Sisters and the surrounding area. For this ride, though, keep riding along the Ponderosa Trail.

The west end of the Sisters Trail takes off to the right at 1.4 miles. Again, stay on the Ponderosa Trail and continue on past the north end of the Silver Fox Trail, which takes off to the right at 1.9 miles. The Silver Fox Trail is a loop that is moderately difficult.

The Ponderosa Trail veers south for 0.5-mile to where it meets the south end of the Silver Fox Trail at 2.4 total miles. Ride the Ponderosa Trail as it turns east to return to the trailhead at 3.1 total miles.

Evergreen Mountain Loop: Difficult; 1–2 hours, 6.3 miles

Park at the east entrance and ride south, across South Buffalo Park Road, and take the only option, the Evergreen Mountain Trail East, to the southeast. At 0.2-mile, the Ranch View Trail takes off to the right, but for this ride stay left on Evergreen Mountain Trail East.

The trail is smooth, well-compacted sand and is not technical for the most part as it climbs up the east side of Evergreen Mountain. As the trail climbs, the forest changes from meadows and ponderosa pine to lodgepole pine at higher elevations.

At 2.5 miles take the Summit Trail to the left. This trail climbs the final 150 feet to the top of Evergreen Mountain. An unnamed overlook trail spurs to the right near the top of the mountain, affording views of the northern sections of the park, including the Three Sisters and the Brother rock outcrops off to the north. At 3.2 total miles the trail splits and makes a loop around the top of the mountain. Go left and ride the 0.7-mile around the loop. There are many views of the surrounding hills (note Pikes Peak to the south) and ranches.

At 3.9 miles the Summit Trail completes the loop. Descend the Summit Trail along the fast single track. *Watch out for hikers on the smooth, fast trail!* At the Evergreen Mountain Trail intersection (mile 4.6) take a left on Evergreen Mountain Trail West. Try to slow before the few switchbacks on the descent (we saw many skid marks heading into the forest from cyclists missing the unexpected sharp corners). Halfway down a sign describes lodgepole pine–thinning projects aimed at reducing the wildfire hazard and increasing habitat in the forest.

At 5.4 miles you will pass the Wild Iris Loop Trail that branches off to the left, and then the Ranch View Trail at 5.6 miles. Cross the road to Evergreen Heights (a housing development in the middle of the park) and continue your descent on the Evergreen Mountain Trail. At 6.1 miles, the East and West Evergreen Mountain Trails merge. Take a left on the Evergreen Mountain Trail and ride the remaining 0.2-mile back to the parking area at 6.3 miles.

SOUTHWESTERN FOOTHILLS AND SUBURBAN PARKS *area*

On the southwestern fringe of the Denver metro area are several open space parks that not only have some challenging trails and fun rides but also allow mountain bikes to use them. Bicycle and pedestrian traffic in many areas can be heavy, so try to avoid peak times, and always use extra caution. Some of the parks also allow horse traffic, so beware, and watch out for horse emissions, which can compromise traction.

Deer Creek Canyon Park

Rating: Difficult to very difficult

Distance: 5–10 miles

Time required: 2–4 hours

Notes: Climbs are steep and technical, but there's a fun loop at the top

Quadrangles: Indian Hills

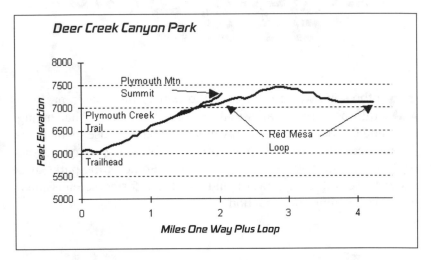

One of the most recent additions to hiking and mountain biking in Jefferson County open space is Deer Creek Canyon Park. The park was first opened in 1995 in one of the most striking small local canyons and leads to some great views. To reach Deer Creek Canyon Park, take C-470 west from I-25 or south from I-70. Take the Kipling exit off of C-470 and head south on Kipling Parkway to West Ute Avenue, which takes off immediately to the right (west). Follow West Ute Avenue for a mile as it heads west then turns south and intersects with Deer Creek Canyon Road. Take a right and head up Deer Creek Canyon Road. Watch for your brethren on road bikes, for this is a popular road-bike ride. Drive up the narrow canyon for

Deer Creek Canyon Park

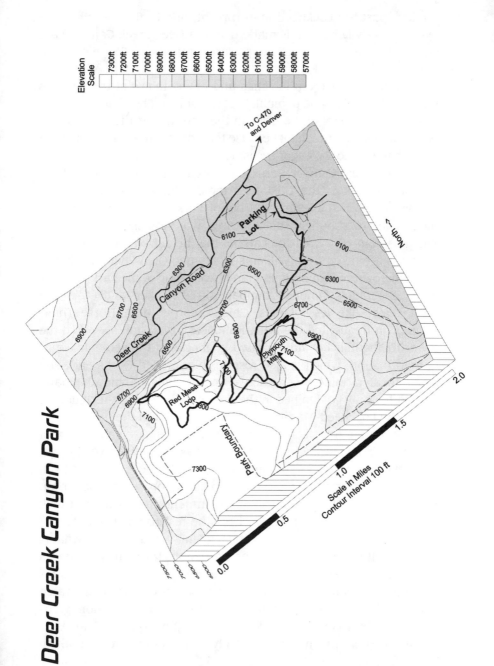

Elevation Scale
7300ft
7200ft
7100ft
7000ft
6900ft
6800ft
6700ft
6600ft
6500ft
6400ft
6300ft
6200ft
6100ft
6000ft
5900ft
5800ft
5700ft

To C-470 and Denver

Parking Lot

North

Deer Creek Canyon Road

Red Mesa Loop

Plymouth Mtn.

Park Boundary

Scale in Miles
Contour Interval 100 ft

0.0   0.5   1.0   1.5   2.0

2 miles, past the Lockheed-Martin plant, and to the turnoff to the left on Grizzly Drive that is marked with a Deer Creek Canyon Park sign. Follow more signs to the parking area about .25-mile up the hill.

There are rest room facilities and picnic tables at the park, as well as a large map and pamphlets at the only trailhead and entrance to the park. Several of the trails in the park are restricted to hiking only, but this is no problem, because the rideable trails are more than enough to satiate the eager cyclist for at least an afternoon.

Deer Creek Canyon Park was originally a campground for nomadic bands of the Ute and Arapaho Indian tribes. It is not known whether the Jefferson County Parks Department charged them a fee to stay here, but the area was homesteaded by John Williamson in 1872, and you can bet that he did. Names of some of the trails are taken from Williamson's famed Glen Plym Ranch and his hometown of Plymouth, England. According to the parks department, Colorado's famous cannibal, Alfred Packer, and other Old West celebs like Jesse James, Chief Colorow, and "Horse Thief" Thompson frequented the area. Ranchers and farmers worked the lower rolling hills behind the tilted hogbacks of the geologic Fountain Formation, which is also responsible for Red Rocks Park and Amphitheater. Mines were active in the hills behind the park, though the only gold mined in the area now is the high-tech dollars sought by Lockheed-Martin at its plant just east of the park.

The nature of Deer Creek Park trails is a combination of smooth, fairly wide single track through oak brush, followed by grueling climbs over rocks that are covered with loose sand and silt, followed by more climbing to the loop at the top, where the terrain has more of a rolling nature. We recommend the Plymouth Creek Trail, which heads off to the left from the rest rooms (6,045 feet in elevation), climbs briefly, then drops, giving you a sense of what is to come. After the first 0.5-mile the trail climbs through switchbacks and then becomes a rocky climb. The rocky ascent continues for about a mile, with only a couple of level spots where you can catch your breath. There is some reprieve from the climb with more gradual grades between the Meadowlark Trail junction at 1.3 miles to where the trail branches, with the Plymouth Mountain Trail taking off to the left and the Plymouth Creek Trail to the right, a half mile later. The Plymouth Mountain Trail is another brutal climb, but only for 0.5-mile. At the top of the climb and the trail spur there is a ridge that connects Plymouth Mountain to the rest of the Front Range. At this point you can take a left and ride another 0.4-mile out to a scenic overlook at the summit of Plymouth Mountain that is actually quite dramatic—if you can focus your eyes, that is—at about 7,250 feet elevation, about 1,200 feet higher than where you started.

Head on over the east side of the ridge on the Plymouth Mountain Trail and begin to descend and wind around the north side of Plymouth Mountain toward the Plymouth Creek Trail that you climbed initially. This descent, as with most descents at Deer Creek Canyon Park, is steep, rough, and, to be honest, a bit dangerous. You must use both brakes and get your butt over the rear wheel, because upon your reaching an uncontrollable speed the rough trail can make it impossible for you to slow down and avoid the large drop-off at the next corner. This is a good place to work on technique (such as tucking your head and rolling as you go over the handlebars!).

When you reach the Plymouth Creek Trail, about 1.5 miles from the trailhead, turn left and continue on the trail for just less than .75-mile over a much more moderate climb with some level stretches to the Red Mesa Loop junction (elevation 7,075 feet). This loop is a great 2.5-mile ride, climbing as high as 7,425 feet in elevation and traversing the side of the canyon, where you can look down hundreds of feet. There are several places on this loop where controlled speed is critical, because the rocky trail, sharp corners, and steep slopes can all cause a great deal of damage to your expensive bike—oh, and to you, too. The country at the top is a picturesque forest with some meadows where deer graze at times. As on all trails, watch for hikers, horses, and other cyclists, especially on descents. This park is a great place to work on climbing and technical descents, as well as endurance if you ride the Red Mesa Loop a few times.

Waterton Canyon/Colorado Trail

Rating: Waterton Road is easy; the trails are difficult to very difficult

Distance: 12–25 miles, or more if you continue on the Colorado Trail

Time required: 2–5 hours

Notes: Waterton Road is a good warm-up or easy family ride; Colorado Trail is a tough workout

Quadrangles: Littleton, Kassler

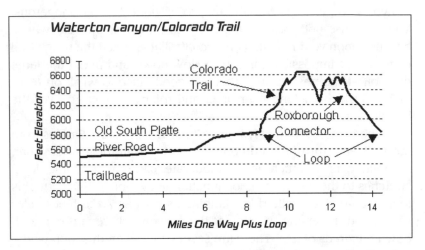

$\mathbf{S}$ outhwest of Denver and just upstream on the South Platte River from Chatfield Reservoir, the old South Platte Road in Waterton Canyon is an easy ride that leads to the Colorado Trail and other much more difficult and technical rides. The Waterton Canyon ride starts in the southernmost end of the Chatfield Reservoir State Recreation Area.

To reach the parking lot and trailhead for Waterton Canyon from Denver, take C-470 south from I-70 or west from I-25 to the Wadsworth Boulevard/Waterton Canyon exit. Head south on Wadsworth (also SH 120) for about 4.5 miles to where a sign indicates that Waterton Park is to the left. The parking lot is to the left

Waterton Canyon/ Colorado Trail

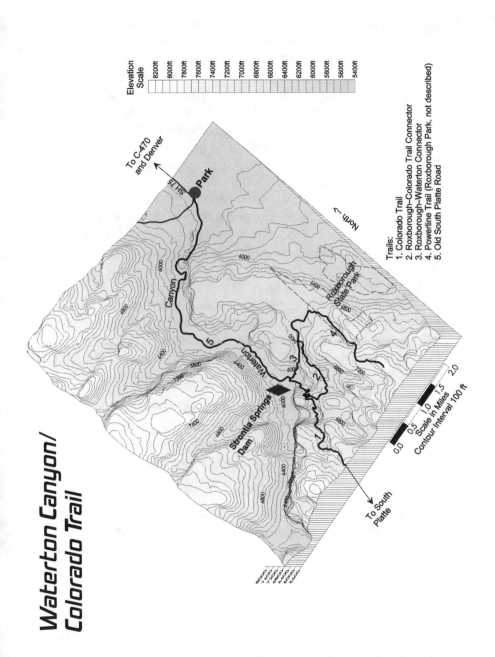

Elevation Scale

8200ft
8000ft
7800ft
7600ft
7400ft
7200ft
7000ft
6800ft
6600ft
6400ft
6200ft
6000ft
5800ft
5600ft
5400ft

To C-470 and Denver

SH 75

Park

Canyon

Waterton

Strontia Springs Dam

Roxborough State Park

North ↑

To South Platte

0.0 0.5 1.0 1.5 2.0
Scale in Miles
Contour Interval 100 ft

Trails:
1. Colorado Trail
2. Roxborough–Colorado Trail Connector
3. Roxborough–Waterton Connector
4. Powerline Trail (Roxborough Park, not described)
5. Old South Platte Road

Waterton Canyon/Colorado Trail ○ 163

immediately after you turn, and the trail crosses the road in front of you as it heads back to the right toward Waterton Canyon.

Mount up at the parking lot and ride west across the road, through some other parking lots, and to the big sign with a map of the park. From here, Old South Platte River Road is a gentle grade along the South Platte River through another scenic canyon displaying striking metamorphic rocks of the Front Range. There are several gravity dams that provide good fishing holes along the way. Bighorn sheep, deer, birds of prey, and other wildlife can be seen along this ride on the canyon walls.

Waterton Canyon is picturesque and a popular place to fish, and many fly rods can be seen strapped to mountain bikes heading up the road. The surface of the road is gravel interspersed with patches of old pavement, though the surface is not too slick. This route is a good place for the whole family, a good recovery ride after an injury, or a good warm up for the more demanding trails farther up.

After 6 miles of riding on the gradually ascending Old South Platte River Road, you will reach Strontia Springs Dam, where the road leaves the South Platte River, heading left (east). As you ride on up the steepening grade you will pass the turnoff to the left for Roxborough State Park and a sign with a map of the trails in the area. Continue riding straight ahead to the Colorado Trail trailhead.

The loop described here is a popular route that starts and ends at the trail map sign. The loop follows the Colorado Trail south to the Roxborough–Colorado Trail Connector, which winds around to the east and north. The ride then turns west on to the Roxborough–Waterton Connector that completes the loop at the area trail map sign mentioned above.

The climb from the trail map sign at the beginning of the loop to the Roxborough–Colorado Trail Connector is a good 1.2-mile climb up a well-groomed single track that has several rideable switchbacks. The junction with the Roxborough–Colorado Trail Connector is marked by a sign and is located at the top of the climb on a saddle ridge that separates Bear Creek to the west and Stevens Gulch to the east. From the junction, you can take a side trip as far as you'd like on the Colorado Trail as it drops down into the Bear Creek drainage and on to the South Platte (6.5 miles).

For the Colorado Trail–Roxborough Connector loop, turn left at the junction. From here the trail climbs a bit on sandy single track and then drops into Stevens Gulch. The descent is somewhat technical and requires good concentration and watching for uphill traffic. Ride for 2.2 miles, meeting a few more climbs and descents, to the junction with the Roxborough–Waterton Connector. Turn left (west) at the sign to return to Waterton Canyon and the beginning of the loop. For another side trip, turn right and ride as far as you like toward Roxborough State Park and return.

The last leg of the loop, the Roxborough–Waterton Connector, is 1 mile long and drops you back near the trail map sign. The route of the Roxborough–Waterton Connector follows the buried water-diversion structure that delivers water from Strontia Springs Reservoir to the suburbs south of Denver and Castle Rock.

This area is very popular, so be courteous on Waterton Road as well as on the Colorado Trail. The Colorado Trail is a multiple-use trail, which means that hikers, horses, and backpackers as well as cyclists may be using this trail at any given time.

RIDES FROM U.S. HIGHWAY 285 *area*

Connecting Denver to south-central Colorado and beyond, U.S. Highway 285 turns into Hampden Avenue upon entering the metro area from the west. It has become something of a commuter route for people living in the southwestern hills and a lot of money has been spent to expand it into a four-lane freeway. But after climbing west up through the Turkey Creek canyon, it becomes a crowded two-way highway. Even so, there are several good places to ride as you climb US 285 over the Front Range, and two very worthy rides are included here.

The history of the route followed by 285 is dominated by that of the railroad. The old railroad grades can still be seen along the highway as you head up Kenosha Pass from Bailey. Railroad men like Jay Gould, John Evans, and Robert J. Spotswood maneuvered for control of this stretch. In 1877 John Evans began the effort of finding a link to the West Coast through the Front Range. The route went up along the South Platte River through the towns of South Platte, Buffalo Creek, and Pine, joining the 285 route at Pine Junction. There were also gold discoveries at Fairplay and coal mines at Como that fueled the interest in this route, but as we now know, the east-west rail corridor ended up going north through the Moffat Tunnel, and another corridor ran through southern Wyoming.

Meyer Ranch Park

Rating: Moderate

Distance: 5.4 miles round-trip as described

Time required: 1–2 hours

Notes: Great scenery and well maintained, but some moderate single track

Quadrangles: Conifer

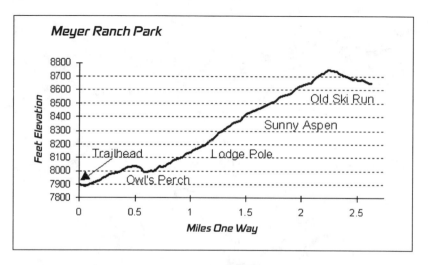

M eyer Ranch Park is a fairly small park just off US 285 about 16 miles southwest of Denver. This park has only 3.75 miles of trail but is still a nice place to pull off and get some climbing in through thick timber. To reach Meyer Ranch Park, head south on US 285 for 16 miles to the junction with South Turkey Creek Road, which comes in from the left (south). In the distance you can see the town of Aspen Park. Be careful turning left here because traffic can be very heavy on this highway. Turn left at the junction and immediately turn right into the parking lot for the park. There is a sign with a park map and other postings and a box holding free maps of the park.

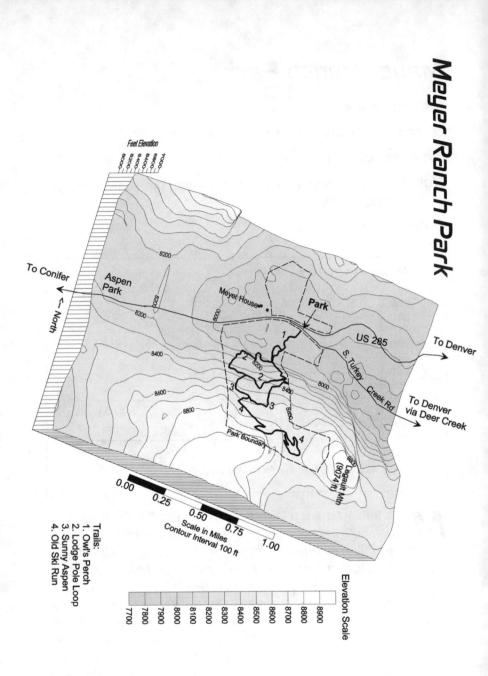

Meyer Ranch Park

Feet Elevation

To Conifer

Aspen Park

Meyer House

Park

US 285

To Denver

S. Turkey Creek Rd

To Denver via Deer Creek

Park Boundary

Legault Mtn (9074 ft)

0.00   0.25   0.50   0.75   1.00
Scale in Miles
Contour Interval 100 ft

Trails:
1. Owl's Perch
2. Lodge Pole Loop
3. Sunny Aspen
4. Old Ski Run

Elevation Scale

7700 7800 7900 8000 8100 8200 8300 8400 8500 8600 8700 8800 8900

Norman and Ethel Meyer, who bought this land and used it for cattle ranching before selling it to Jefferson County, started Meyer Ranch in 1950. The Meyers still live in the house just to the north across US 285. A man named Duncan McIntyre first homesteaded the land and, according to Jefferson County, it is rumored that P. T. Barnum used this area as a wintering spot for his circus between 1880 and 1890. This is corroborated by Norman Meyer's discovery of a sign that read "Circus Town 1889" when he was renovating his house.

Old Ski Run Trail in the park actually was a ski run at one time, and you can imagine that this slope would hold snow quite well, because it is facing almost due north. The ski run dates to the 1940s and was not outfitted with lifts.

Begin riding at the Owl's Perch trailhead (7,890 feet in elevation) for 0.3-mile past the rest rooms to where the trail splits at a picnic area. You can go right or left, because the trails soon rejoin at 0.4-mile. No sooner does this happen, though, when they split up again into the Lodge Pole Loop. Take a right at this split and ride for 0.6-mile across and up the slope with one switchback to another trail junction. If you keep going straight you can finish the Lodge Pole Loop. But for now turn right on Sunny Aspen Trail and climb up the slope for another 0.3-mile for a total of 1.3 miles to another junction and picnic area. At this point you will be at 8,330 feet in elevation, a net gain of 440 feet.

Take another right at this junction and head for the top of the park on Old Ski Run Trail. This trail winds up through the timber and climbs to 8,650 feet in elevation in .75-mile to where it splits and makes a 0.6-mile loop, reaching nearly 8,750 feet in elevation. The recommended route is to ride the loop at the top and head back down Old Ski Run Trail, then turn right (east) on Sunny Aspen Trail and ride for 0.6-mile, then turn left (west) on Lodge Pole Loop Trail and ride the loop all the way around for 1 mile and back to Owl's Perch Trail, where you started, in order to get the most out of the small park.

Colorado Trail at Kenosha Pass

Rating: Difficult to very difficult

Distance: 24 miles round-trip

Time required: 2–4 hours

Notes: Great scenery and well maintained but tough single track

Quadrangles: Boreas Pass, Jefferson

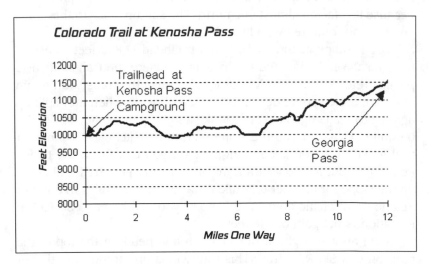

*T*ravel on US 285 south out of Denver for about 50 miles, past Conifer and Bailey. At the crest of Kenosha Pass (10,000 feet in elevation) is Kenosha Campground and a trailhead for the Colorado Trail. You can park either at the campground or along the highway. Ride into the campground and follow the signs to the Colorado Trail. This ride has several alternative routes because it crosses roads, travels near campgrounds, and branches into other trails. The route described here heads west on the Colorado Trail to the top of Georgia Pass (11,585 feet in elevation), and then back for a round-trip.

This route is a popular place in the autumn (mid-September),

Colorado Trail at Kenosha Pass

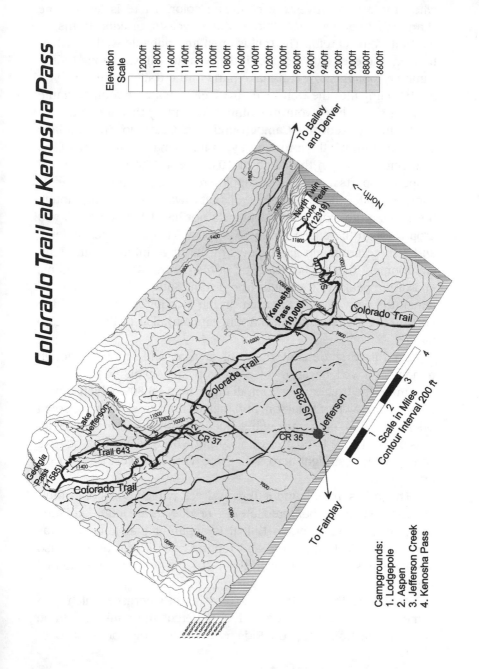

Elevation Scale

12000ft
11800ft
11600ft
11400ft
11200ft
11000ft
10800ft
10600ft
10400ft
10200ft
10000ft
9800ft
9600ft
9400ft
9200ft
9000ft
8800ft
8600ft

To Bailey and Denver

North

North Twin Cone Peak (12319)

Shag Tun

Kenosha Pass (10,000)

Colorado Trail

US 285

Jefferson

Georgia Pass (11585)

Trail 643

Lake Jefferson

CR 37

CR 35

Colorado Trail

To Fairplay

Scale in Miles
0 1 2 3 4
Contour Interval 200 ft

Campgrounds:
1. Lodgepole
2. Aspen
3. Jefferson Creek
4. Kenosha Pass

when the aspen groves are changing color. There is always the chance that you will meet hikers, other cyclists, or equestrians on the trail, so be careful. The trail is open and rideable well into September, and even into October if the weather allows a long Indian summer, though snow can make parts of the trail sloppy. So if you are traveling into the Denver metro area to watch a football game or other event, bring your mountain bike and try this ride out.

From the Kenosha Campground, the Colorado Trail initially climbs up through the forest, and your lungs may remind you of the fact that you began the climb at 10,000 feet. The trail is in good shape but sports many power-sapping roots throughout the ride. At about 1.5 miles the trail finally drops off toward South Park, though not leaving the slopes that define its northeast boundary. As you drop through the aspen and across rocky slopes between miles 2 and 3 there are some great views of the huge intermontane park environment that is characteristic of the central Rocky Mountains, and of the peaks to the south (the distant Sangre de Cristo Mountains), the west (Mount Sherman in the Mosquito Range), and the north (Mount Democrat and Mount Lincoln, also in the Mosquito Range).

On this first descent the trail is nice and smooth, though remember it well, because you will climb back up on the return trip. At 3 miles the trail crosses a small ditch, then FS 809, which comes up from the town of Jefferson, and then a small creek running down Guernsey Gulch on a narrow but rideable bridge—all in quick succession. You have to be pretty good to ride bridges like this, so take care. Continue straight across all three, continue west on the Colorado Trail.

The Jefferson Trail and Jefferson Creek (which flows out of Jefferson Lake) are encountered later in the ride, as are Jefferson Creek Campground and Jefferson Hill. It is apparent that Jefferson was very popular in these parts, and reports have it that he was also twenty points ahead of Dole in this district in the 1996 presidential election.

Aspen are thick at the creek crossing at Guernsey Gulch, and some have fallen as the creek has undercut the bank, the same bank that the trail is now on. Ride on through clumps of aspen, over

A view of the Georgia Pass area from the Colorado Trail, near Kenosha Pass.

more roots that are forced to creep just below the surface of the ground because of the rocky glacial soil, to Deadman Creek at 4.5 miles. This creek crossing is technical because of large rocks and roots that take some skill to ride. At 4.8 miles the trail joins an old unnamed road for a short stretch, then turns sharply to the left at 5 miles, so be ready to continue on it.

At 5.8 miles the Colorado Trail passes through a Forest Service gate that is to be kept shut for livestock management, and the trail continues to wind around the north end of South Park to where it crosses CR 37 and Jefferson Creek at 6 miles. If you have trouble or an injury, CR 37 can provide a bailout to the town of Jefferson, which is about 7 miles to the south. Upon crossing CR 37 you are halfway to the summit of Georgia Pass, but there is plenty of climbing yet to come.

After crossing CR 37 the trail climbs again for .25-mile to a junction, marked by signs, with the Jefferson Trail (FS Trail 643). Turn right (north) and ride up the Jefferson/Colorado Trail, which follows an abandoned road toward Jefferson Creek Campground. In only about 0.1-mile, there is a fork where the Colorado Trail takes off to the left and up the hill toward Georgia Pass. At this point you can take either trail to the top of Georgia Pass.

If you continue to Jefferson Creek Campground, Jefferson Trail will take you to Georgia Pass after about 6 miles, meeting back up with the Colorado Trail about a mile from the summit, and you can actually make a loop out of this. This portion of the route is less well maintained and there are more bridges over small creeks. These bridges are constructed of two aspen logs tied together and laid over the creek. They are not rideable. Jefferson Trail follows Jefferson Creek up most of the way and is technical in places, very technical in others, and smooth in a few spots. One advantage of Jefferson Trail is that it will not be very crowded.

The recommended route is to take the Colorado Trail, which heads west and climbs over the small divide from Jefferson Creek to Ohler Gulch, where it turns and heads north to the summit. The trail is rocky and with roots from the pine, spruce, and fir that have surrounded you since you crossed Jefferson Creek and entered the montane ecosystem. From the Jefferson Trail it is 5.5 miles and about 1,500 feet of climbing on the Colorado Trail to the summit of Georgia Pass. The reward of all this climbing is that there is a long, though rough, downhill back to Jefferson Creek, where you have to climb back to Kenosha Pass.

Upon reaching the summit of Georgia Pass it is best to return via the Colorado Trail because it is a better trail than the Jefferson Trail. Either way, make sure you get on the Colorado Trail at the Colorado/Jefferson Trails junction south of Jefferson Campground. From there, return the way you came. The total one-way length of the ride to Georgia Pass is 12 miles—a bit longer, about 12.5 miles, if you take the Jefferson Trail.

Buffalo Creek Mountain Bike Area

Rating: Moderate to very difficult

Distance: 5–25 miles

Time required: 2–5 hours

Notes: Lots of trails to choose from; campgrounds close by; a popular fishing area

Quadrangles: Pine, Platte Canyon, Green Mountain, Deckers

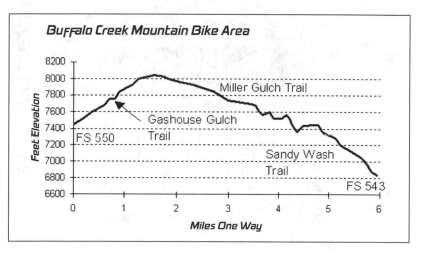

The Buffalo Creek Mountain Bike Area is a popular place to ride because it has a wide variety of trails open to mountain bikes. The area was, however, affected in May of 1996 by careless campers who started a forest fire that scorched over 11,000 acres and closed several trails. In addition, the area was scorched by several small fires started by lightning in June of the same year.

Not long after the fires the misfortunes of the area took yet another bad turn. Flash floods hit the area, washing out the highway and taking out several houses and buildings in the town of Buffalo Creek. There were several other flash-floods during the summer of 1996, though none was as potent as the first. This is a similar scenario to that experienced at the infamous Storm King

Buffalo Creek Mountain Bike Area

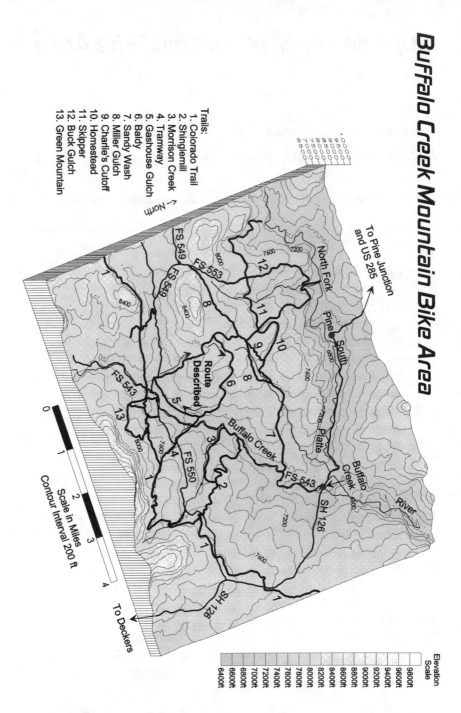

Trails:
1. Colorado Trail
2. Shinglemill
3. Morrison Creek
4. Tramway
5. Gashouse Gulch
6. Baldy
7. Sandy Wash
8. Miller Gulch
9. Charlie's Cutoff
10. Homestead
11. Skipper
12. Buck Gulch
13. Green Mountain

← North

Elevation Scale
9800ft
9600ft
9400ft
9200ft
9000ft
8800ft
8600ft
8400ft
8200ft
8000ft
7800ft
7600ft
7400ft
7200ft
7000ft
6800ft
6600ft
6400ft

Scale in Miles
Contour Interval 200 ft

To Pine Junction and US 285

To Deckers

Mountain fire near Glenwood Springs, Colorado, where heavy summer rains followed forest fires. In the Buffalo Creek area, erosion and runoff was enhanced by the lack of soil-stabilizing vegetation, though the effects of the floodwaters on structures near the channel would have been severe anyway because the gravelly floodplains have a tendency to be washed away during high water. The highways in the area were also victims of this phenomenon, as the rapidly moving water made easy work of eroding the soil that the road was constructed with. Large rocks, or riprap, are piled along the sides of river channels to help to prevent this kind of thing. This highway has since been repaired.

Most of the area open to mountain biking is located northwest of the burned area and west of the area that was flooded. Most of the damaged trails have been or will be reopened at some point, but it is a good idea to contact the Pike National Forest South Platte Ranger District before covering the 50 miles from Denver to get there (303-236-5371).

Despite the dynamic natural processes, mountain bikers should not overlook this area. The following descriptions apply to the trails as they were just before the fires occurred. Through restoration efforts by the Forest Service these trails are again rideable, though they're not as easy as they once were, due to the large amounts of sand that have washed down across them in places.

The terrain in the Buffalo Creek area is fairly rugged, and many of the trails gain a great deal of elevation. Riding some of the unimproved roads in the area provides an easier workout. Most years the Buffalo Creek Classic mountain bike race, sponsored by the Sunburst Cycling Club, is held on one of the loops in the area, starting near the Buffalo Creek Campground. So check it out if you like to see what kind of bike a grand or so can fetch.

To reach Buffalo Creek, take US 285 south from Denver for about 20 miles to Pine Junction and turn left (south) on SH 126. This road winds as it drops down into the Platte River Valley for about 20 miles to the town of Pine. About 5 miles farther you will reach the town of Buffalo Creek. Both of these towns were important whistle-stops during the expansion of railroads into the Front Range. The road between Pine and Buffalo Creek is very picturesque as it follows the

North Fork of the South Platte River. Pine Valley Road from Pine Junction to Buffalo Creek is a good road-bike ride as well.

At Buffalo Creek, FS 543 takes off to the right, leading into the Buffalo Creek Mountain Bike Area. About 5 miles farther, on SH 126, FS 550 takes off to the right (west), entering the south side of the Buffalo Creek Mountain Bike Area. Trails can be accessed from either of these roads or others within the area, and camping is available at Buffalo, Meadows, Tramway, Green Mountain, or Baldy campgrounds, though Meadows is reserved for groups.

Both FS 543 and FS 550 are normally in pretty good shape, though both are narrow and with hairpin turns and blind spots, and with washboards and potholes in the gravel roads. Unless you get caught in a prolonged rainstorm or are here out of season, the roads are passable in a normal passenger car.

Most of the area is located on Pikes Peak granite, a brown to pink igneous rock that is found from here to south of Pikes Peak. This rock weathers into rounded rock outcrops and produces a lot of sand and fine gravel rubble. This combination produces an interesting landscape, and the loose material can make riding tricky in places.

On some downhill stretches bikes have created ruts and what appear to be banked turns due to the tires pushing sand to the outside of turns. The banks are not stable, however, and getting caught in the deep sand at the edges of turns can send you tumbling. If you are a less experienced cyclist you will probably take the downhills at a conservative speed, but if you live for watching *Downhill-mania* or the *X-Games* on ESPN2, I suggest hooking your brakes back up before heading into this area.

Many of the trails in the Buffalo Creek Mountain Bike Area feature blind hairpin turns that are preceded by potholes created by bikes skidding in panic as the pilot realizes he has far more inertia than his coefficient of friction with the ground can hope to redirect. These potholes create a real problem even for fully suspended bikes, and skidding only makes the problem worse and causes more wear and tear on the area. So, please, take it easy and enjoy the ride.

There are so many rides in the area that it would be laborious

A boulder-y Gashouse Gulch Trail in the Buffalo Creek Mountain Bike Area.

to describe them all. All of the rideable trails are shown on the map and illustrate typical rides in the central part of the area. A very popular 5.7-mile loop is to start at the Buffalo campground and ride on up Forest Service Road 550 to the west for a little over half a mile and turn right (north) on an unimproved and unnamed road that climbs up the hill to join the Gashouse Gulch Trail.

After about .25-mile you will reach a gate where the road ends and the Gashouse Gulch Trail comes in from the right, then turns and heads off to the north ahead of you. Start your odometer here. Continuing straight ahead through a gate in the pole fence, climb onward and upward. The trail is technical in spots, though it's just a good climb over most of it. There are several places where you have to climb up a steep grade while turning sharply (this skill is handy and will be tested on many trails in the area). Follow Gashouse Gulch Trail for 1.5 miles over the top of the hill to where it becomes much easier and widens, joining the Baldy Trail. Turn right on Baldy Trail and descend, getting a much-deserved breather. Some of the more challenging downhill stretches are on the next

2.7 miles of trail, so concentrate and enjoy the downhill, because there is another good climb back up to the end of the loop. At 4.2 miles the Baldy Trail reaches the Gashouse Gulch Trail once again, just west of where Baldy Trail joins FS 543. Take a right and climb on to the Gashouse Gulch Trail and wind gradually to the west. The trail straightens, and at 5.7 miles you reach the beginning of the loop.

Ride this loop as many times as you'd like, or expand it by following the Gashouse Gulch Trail to the north, past the Baldy Trail turnoff, to the Miller Gulch Trail and looping back around from the east or west. The loop to the east joins FS 543 and makes for a 12-mile loop if you start and end at Buffalo Campground.

Other rides in the Buffalo Creek Mountain Bike Area include the Colorado Trail along the south end of the area; the Buck Gulch, Skipper, and Homestead Trails in the northern end; and the Shingle Mill and Morrison Creek Trails in the east of the area. All of these trails are moderate rides with difficult sections. The easiest trails are at the west end of the Miller Gulch Trail starting from FS 553 and FS 543.

Something else to note is that the Colorado Trail, which traverses the south end of the area, crossing FS 550 near SH 126, then crossing SH 126 at a marked trailhead about 1 mile north of the junction with FS 550, connects with Waterton Canyon, described on page 162. From SH 126 it is 9 miles of moderate and difficult trail to the South Platte, then 7 miles of moderate and difficult trail that includes some grueling climbs to the Roxborough–Colorado Trail Connector (see page 164). Another 1.2 miles of moderate downhill gets you to the end of the old South Platte Road and Waterton Canyon.

APPENDIX: A LIST OF BIKE SHOPS IN THE COLORADO FRONT RANGE

*T*he following is a list of the bike stores in the area covered by this book and who agreed to be listed. We didn't include all of the stores, but tried to select those located near or on the way to rides.

Arvada

Arvada Bicycle Co.
6595 Wadsworth Boulevard
80003 (303) 420-3854

Bicycle Center, The
6390 Wadsworth Boulevard
80003 (303) 423-3095

Bicycles Flow
5650 Olde Wadsworth Blvd.
80002 (303) 940-6463

Cycle Madness
9422 W. 58th Avenue
80002 (303) 431-6388

Foothills Schwinn
11651 Ralston Road
80004 (303) 420-0815

Aurora

Adventure Cycling
4361 S. Parker Road
Denver 80015
699-2514

Bicycle Village East
15280 East Iliff Avenue
80014-4516
(303) 369-9090

Bike Path
15353 East 6th Avenue
80011-9001 (303) 363-8800

Buckley Bicycles
16981 East Iliff Avenue
80013-1587 (303) 750-1671

Smokey Hill Cyclery
15250 East Hampden Avenue
80014-3908 (303) 680-0442

Boulder

Bicycle Center, The
2624 Broadway
80304-3452 (303) 442-1832

Bicycle Village
1681 28th Street
80301-1001 (303) 440-8525

Boulder Bikesmith
3864 Campo Court
80301-1793 (303) 443-1132

Doc's Ski and Sports
627 South Broadway
80303-5926 (303) 499-0963

Excel Sports Boulder
2045 32nd Street
80301-2501 (303) 444-6737

Full Cycle
1211 13th Street
80302-7017 (303) 440-7771

Gecko Cycles
7209 Valtec Court
80301-4626 (303) 786-7120

Loco Caramba Cycles
6395 Gunpark Drive
80301-3390 (303) 530-4953

Performance Bicycle Shop
2490 Arapahoe Avenue
80302-6709 (303) 444-5044

University Bicycles
839 Pearl Street
80302-5007 (303) 444-4196

Broomfield

Bicycle Village
7743 West 92nd Avenue
80021-8609 (303) 421-4001

Hillside Cyclery
11965 Pierce Street
80020-2947 (303) 466-7731

Castle Rock

Castle Rock Cyclery
302 Wilcox Street
80104-2441 (303) 660-6155

Life Cycle
217 4th Street
80104-2410 (303) 688-8086

Colorado Springs

Bike Habit
1812 Dominion Way
80918-1467 (719) 599-0707

Colorado Cyclist
3970 East Bijou Street
80909 (719) 591-4045

Colorado Mountain Bike Source
806 Arcturus Drive
80906-1833 (719) 632-8459

Colorado Springs Bike Shop
3940 Palmer Park Boulevard
80909-3404 (719) 597-8782

Colorado Springs Bike Shop
622 West Colorado Avenue
80905-1513 (719) 634-4915

Criterium Bike Shops, Inc.
5660 North Academy Boulevard
80918-3659 (719) 599-0149

Criterium Bike Shops, Inc.
326 North Tejon Street
80903-1224 (719) 475-0149

Cycle Therapy
6975 North Academy Boulevard
80918 (719) 590-8889

Cycle Therapy
3365 North Academy Boulevard
80917-5103 (719) 596-8804

Cyclo-Rays'
1138 East Fillmore Street
80907-6318 (719) 442-0631

Gilbert's Cycles
415 Juanita Street
80909-6234 (719) 634-5791

Grand West Outfitters
3250 North Academy Boulevard
80917 (719) 598-7988

Ketu Cycles
806 Village Center Drive
80919-3603 (719) 598-7988

National Off-Road Bicycle
  Association
One Olympic Plaza
80909 (719) 578-4581

Old Town Bike Shop
2409 West Colorado Avenue
80904-3021 (719) 475-8589

Pedal Revolution, The
1803 East Boulder Street
80909-5725 (719) 389-0909

Pedersen's Ski & Sports
750 Citadel Drive West
80909-5353 (719) 574-6199

Rocky Mountain Bikes & Blades
3647 Star Ranch Road
80906-5980 (719) 527-0427

Rocky Mountain High Wheels
1803 East Boulder Street
80909-5725 (719) 633-3538

Ski Smith
815 North Nevada Avenue
80903 (719) 636-2340

Teds Bicycle, Inc.
3016 North Hancock Avenue
80907-5711 (719) 473-6915

Commerce City

Derby Bicycle Shop
7240 Locust Street
80022-1735 (303) 288-4100

Copper Mountain

Christy Sports
230 Ten Mile Circle
(970) 968-6250

Denver

A C Lawnmower & Bicycle
  Shop
2374 South Downing Street
80210-5810 (303) 733-2331

American Cyclery
2140 South Albion Street
80222-4904 (303) 756-1023

Bicycle Doctor, The
860 Broadway
80203-2704 (303) 831-7228

Bicycle Village
6300 East Colfax Avenue
80220-1602 (303) 355-5339

Big Wheel Ltd.
7150 Leetsdale Drive
80224-3516 (303) 333-2449

Bike Broker, Inc.
1440 Market Street
80202-1707 (303) 893-8675

Bike Lovers' Place
7400 East Hampden Avenue
80231-4803 (303) 740-7161

Campus Cycles
1730 East Evans Avenue
80210-4602 (303) 698-2811

Collins Bicycles
3217 East Colfax Avenue
80206-1711 (303) 322-1786

Cycle Analyst, Inc.
722 South Pearl Street
80209-4213 (303) 722-3004

Denver Bicycle Werx
6336 Leetsdale Drive
80224-1261 (303) 399-2453

Denver Spoke
1715 East Evans Avenue
80210-4601 (303) 777-1720

Dragon Lowriders
975 Santa Fe Drive
80204-3936 (303) 615-9050

Greentree Cyclery
1549 South Pearl Street
80210-2634 (303) 777-4518

Main Frame Bicycle Shop, Inc.
2520 Sheridan Boulevard
80214-3017 (303) 480-9280

Mile High Bicycles
3989 East 120th Avenue
80233-1662 (303) 254-8113

Mojo Wheels II
5790 West Dartmouth Avenue
80227-5505 (303) 985-4487

Mojo Wheels, Inc.
1978 South Garrison Street
80227-2243 (303) 986-8216

My Brother's Bicycle
10015 East Hampden Avenue
80231-4904 (303) 671-5511

Northglenn Bicycle Shop
842 East 120th Avenue
80233-1201 (303) 451-7733

Performance Bicycle Shop
2540 South Colorado Boulevard
80222-5909 (303) 756-7734

Premier Cycles of Cherry Creek
2406 East 3rd Avenue
80206-4704 (303) 331-9502

Recreational Equipment, Inc.
  (REI)
4100 East Mexico Avenue
(800) 222-4100

Schwab Cycles
1565 Pierce Street
80214-1421 (303) 238-0243

Special Offer Bicycle Repair
7036 East Colfax Avenue
80220-1804 (303) 333-2453

Steve's Cycle Works
(303) 433-1230

Street Sports
4521 Leetsdale Drive
80222-1214 (303) 394-3719

Turin Bicycles Ltd.
700 Lincoln Street
80203-3416 (303) 837-1857

Dillon

Mogul Mikes of Dillon
101 Village Place
(970) 468-5506

Englewood

Alpha Bicycle Company
6838 South Yosemite Street
80112-1407 (303) 220-9799

Bike Line of Greenwood Village
4968 South Yosemite Street
80111-1309 (303) 771-0903

Bikes & Berries
69 West Floyd Avenue
80110-2420 (303) 781-6225

Englewood Bicycle Company
3546 South Logan Street
80110-3731 (303) 781-1162

Estes Park

Colorado Bicycling Adventures
184 East Elkhorn Avenue
(970) 586-4241

Evergreen

Bike Shop Bills
6949 Highway 73
80439-6200 (303) 674-8199

Canyon Cycles
29289 Highway 74
(303) 670-2728

Paragon Sports Ltd.
2962 Evergreen Parkway
80439 (303) 670-0092

Fort Collins

A-1 Bike City
410 Jefferson Street
80524 (970) 484-8667

Bike Broker, Inc.
152 West Mountain Avenue
80524-2823 (970) 484-2453

Bike City
740 Daisy Street
80521-3532 (970) 224-1609

Bike Works, Inc.
1725 South College Avenue
80525-1008 (970) 224-3013

Bikesmith, The
1213 West Elizabeth Street
80521-4508 (970) 224-4840

Catamount Cycles Retail
    Showroom
517 North Link Lane
80524-2737 (970) 493-8315

Cycle Transport, Inc.
(Campus Location)
650 South College Avenue
80524-3004 (970) 221-2869

Cycletote Corp.
517 North Link Lane
80524-2737 (970) 482-2401

Freewheeler, The
1205 West Elizabeth Street
80521-4562 (970) 224-3262

Lee's Cyclery
931 East Harmony Road
80524-4871 (970) 226-6006

Lee's Cyclery
202 West Laurel Street
80525-2809 (970) 482-6006

Pedersen's Ski & Sports
Foothills Fashion Mall
(970) 223-4757

Recycled Cycles-Total Fitness,
    Inc.
4031 South Mason Street
80525-3053 (970) 223-1969

Recreational Equipment, Inc.
    (REI)
4025 South College Avenue
80525-3039 (970) 223-0123

Rockn Road Cyclery
4206 South College Avenue
80525-3019 (970) 223-7623

Together Tandems
2030 South College Avenue
80524-1425 (970) 224-0330

Wayne's Bicycle
346 East Mountain Avenue
80524-2914 (970) 482-4970

Fort Morgan

Bicycle Livery, The
531 Main Street
80701-2131 (970) 867-2941

Frisco

Cyclesmiths
418 Main
(970) 668-1385

Golden

Apex Mountain Sports
18301 West Colfax Avenue
80401-4834 (303) 278-4268

Granby

Grand Cycle
250 East Agate Avenue
(970) 887-9449

Greeley

Cycle Logic
3820 10th Street
80634-1526 (970) 356-3663

International Bike
2529 11th Avenue
80631-6927 (970) 353-8575

International Bike
2812 10th Street
80631-3425 (970) 352-6989

Idaho Springs

Mountain & Road Bicycle
   Repair
1514 Miner
(303) 567-4666

Lafayette

Cycletherapy
550 West South Boulder Road
80026-8824 (303) 666-9303

Lakewood

Bicycle Village West
305 South Kipling Street
80226-2700 (303) 988-3210

Bike Station
10041 West 26th Avenue
80215-6656 (303) 238-1797

Gene's Bicycle & Lawn Mower
   Service
6625 West Mississippi Avenue
80226-4634 (303) 922-1562

Performance Bicycle Shop
11058 West Jewell Avenue
80232-6120 (303) 987-1376

Premier Bicycles of Lakewood
98 Wadsworth Boulevard
80226-1550 (303) 935-7550

Westside Schwinn
7310 West Colfax Avenue
80215-4115 (303) 237-1115

Littleton

Antique Wheels Unlimited
(303) 795-9424

Arapahoe Cyclery
6905 South Broadway
80122-8000 (303) 797-1858

Bicycle Village
10201 West Bowles Avenue
80217-2037 (303) 978-9699

Bicycle Village South
6810 South University
   Boulevard
80122-1515 (303) 740-0900

Littleton Cyclery & Fitness
1500 West Littleton Boulevard
80120-2103 (303) 798-5033

Pedal n' Pleasure
9032 West Ken Caryl Avenue
80123-5250 (303) 973-8901

Pedersen's Ski & Sports
8501 West Bowles Avenue
80123-3245 (303) 932-0006

Premier Cycles South
7680 South University
  Boulevard
80122-3145 (303) 796-0185

Recreational Equipment, Inc.
  (REI)
5375 South Wadsworth
  Boulevard
80123-2229 (303) 932-0600

Tandem Cycle Works
5435 Mohawk Road
80123-2940 (303) 795-5611

Wheel Estate
2030 East County Line Road
80126-2403 (303) 730-8038

Longmont

Bike Route Bicycles
1801 Hover Road
80501-7182 (303) 772-0209

Bike-N-Hike
1136 Main Street
80501-3823 (303) 772-5105

High Gear Cyclery, Inc.
1834 Main Street
80501-2066 (303) 772-4327

Louisville

Louisville Cyclery
1032 East South Boulder Road
80027-2529 (303) 665-6343

Superior Bicycles & Fitness
368 South McCaslin Boulevard
80027-9432 (303) 665-7244

Loveland

Dr. Spoke Bicycle Shoppe
280 East 29th Street
80538-2733 (970) 663-0944

Loveland Cycle n' Fitness
524 Cleveland Avenue
80537-5510 (970) 667-1943

Peloton Cycles
126 East 29th Street
80538-2724 (970) 669-5595

Monument

Cycle Therapy
1754 Lake Woodmoor Drive
80132-9074 (719) 488-8804

Parker

Destination Cyclery
17930 Cottonwood Drive
80134-3951 (303) 690-2900

Parker Bikes
10841 South Crossroads Drive
80134-9081 (303) 841-8551

Westminster

Pedersen's Ski & Sports
Westminster Mall
(303) 650-5967

Recreational Equipment, Inc.
  (REI)
8991 Harlan Street
80030-2931 (303) 429-1800

Wheat Ridge

Wheat Ridge Cyclery
7085 West 38th Avenue
80033-4836 (303) 424-3221

Woodland Park

Angletech
318 State Highway 67
80863-1046 (719) 687-7475

GLOSSARY OF
MOUNTAIN BIKE TERMINOLOGY

Bonk. Oh, please! Let's be adults here. It means that you didn't consume enough food on a long ride, causing your blood sugar levels to drop dangerously low. This results in disorientation and loss of coordination.

Bottom bracket. The part of the bike frame and bearing assembly that provides the housing for the crank-set spindle. If you have regular (not a sealed-cartridge-bearing assembly) ball bearings, they will need adjusting and repacking often after hard or wet riding.

Burner. A climb that is very strenuous, making your legs burn before you get to the top.

Chain ring. The gears on the crank that drive the chain as you pedal.

Chain slap. When the chain slaps against the chain stay, a phenomenon caused by going over bumps while coasting. Prevent this by shifting into the largest front chain ring.

Chain stay. The part of the bike frame that connects the bottom bracket to the rear wheel.

Chain suck. When the chain sticks to the front chain ring and gets pulled up between the ring and the chain stay, usually causing damage to the chain and binding it up. This usually occurs in the lowest gear and the least opportune situations; keeping the chain clean and well lubricated can help to prevent this problem, as can special devices that can be fixed to the chain stay.

Crank set. The two crank arms that connect the pedals to the spindle. Can also include the chain rings.

Cross-shift. A situation in which the front chain ring on which the chain is engaged doesn't match well with the rear. An example would be riding in the largest front ring and the largest rear ring or the smallest in front and smallest in rear. This causes the chain to have to bend to reach the rear gear, causing undue wear on the chain.

Derailleur. The device that shifts gears on either the front chain rings or the rear gear cluster by moving the chain from sprocket to sprocket. The rear derailleur is a common casualty when branches get pulled into it by the chain.

Digger. To come into contact with the ground or another stationary object when you are traveling at high speeds, possibly causing bodily injury.

Dog on a Walk.* A fast rider with a slow-rider companion whom the fast rider is always going back to check on.

Dropped. Left behind by another cyclist while cycling due to differences in speed or effort.

Endo. A truncated conjunction that evolved from *end-over-end*, a term referring to the motion that a bicycle and rider undergo when the front wheel is abruptly decelerated. The result is the rider is tossed over the handlebars to an unknown fate.

Fancy lad.* A cyclist decked out in all the newest gear and riding an expensive bike.

Folded. The damage inflicted on a bicycle frame, typically during an endo, in which the down tube is bent inward by the stress from the fork and the top tube collapses under tension.

Front wheelie. A controlled endo caused by locking the front brake at a low speed and lifting the rear wheel off the ground.

Get air. To jump into the air off a small hill or bump in the trail while cycling.

Gonzo. A state of being very aggressive on downhills; lacking concern for one's well-being while cycling.

Gonzo-abusive. A trail that is very tough and possibly dangerous if one were to crash.

Gripped. Feelings of fright on very technical sections. Usage: *I was completely gripped on that tight hairpin above the 100-foot cliff.*

Hammer. To push really hard until your legs burn and you finally finish a ride or climb thoroughly exhausted. A *hammerhead* is someone who hammers a lot.

Knobbies. Off-road tires.

Line. A course or route taken through a technical stretch of trail.

Portage. To carry your bike through an unrideable section.

Potato chip a wheel. Verb construction; *see* Wheel taco.

Pushing a gear. Riding up a hill in a gear that is too high and thus too hard to pedal. If you make it to the top you may be too tired to ride the next hill.

Put a Band-Aid on it.* Get up, stop whining, and keep riding.

Swag (pronounced "shwag"). To cyclists, this means cool free stuff you get from a product sponsor. Others consider it a term with a negative connotation.

Self-composting pit toilet.* A toilet type used in Jefferson County parks that promotes the biodegradation of human wastes. The toilets have no odor and are very clean.

Slicks. Smooth tires for mountain bikes, for extended road travel, or for trails such as those on slick rock in Moab, Utah. *Note:* They don't look nearly as cool around town as knobbies do.

Snake-bite. Two small holes in a tire tube resembling the holes made by rattlesnake fangs. They are caused by pinching the tube between the wheel rim and a rock or other sharp object. This happens when a bike runs over a sharp or angular solid object. It's exacerbated by low tire pressures.

Technical. A trail with boulders or cobbles, a steep grade, a slick surface, or all of the above. Technical trails require good balance and strength and can be dangerous if there is a large drop-off nearby.

Techno-weenie. A cyclist who purchases all of the best high-tech, lightweight equipment and components, but doesn't really ride that much.

Thrash. To travel downhill at an unreasonable speed, which can be the maximum speed attainable before catastrophic failure and crashing is imminent. Syn.: *gonzo.*

Water bar. A water-diversion structure composed of a berm of soil that is graded up across a trail or road.

Wheel taco. The result after a crash that applies unusual lateral stress on the bicycle's front wheel, bending it into a U-shape in profile. This can be fixed enough to ride (or limp) home, but normally it ruins the rim and spokes. Syn.: *Potato chip a wheel.*

Yuppie garage ornament. * An expensive full-suspension bicycle that is rarely ridden.

*First documented here as cycling lingo. We take no responsibility for the consequences of using these terms.

BIBLIOGRAPHY AND RECOMMENDED READING

Brown, Robert L. *Central City and Gilpin County: Then and Now.* Caldwell, Idaho: The Caxton Printers, Ltd., 1994.

Chronic, Halka. *Roadside Geology of Colorado (Roadside Geology Series)*. Missoula, Montana: Mountain Press Publishing Company, 1986.

McTighe, James. *Roadside History of Colorado.* Revised edition. Boulder, Colorado: Johnson Books, 1989

INDEX